Historic Sites
of
County Durham

Glen Lyndon Dodds

Albion
Press

Albion Press
40 Park Parade Roker Sunderland Tyne & Wear
©1996
ISBN 0 9525122 5 4

British Library Cataloguing in Publication Data.
A catalogue record for this book is available from the British Library

Cover: The west towers of Durham Cathedral
viewed from the River Wear

Designed and typeset by Gavin Dodds
using the Commodore Amiga
Printed and bound in Great Britain by
Biddles Limited Woodbridge Park
Guildford Surrey GU1 1DA

CONTENTS

For Linda and Julie

PREFACE

M uch of the material in this book has been derived from an unpublished work entitled *The Historic River Wear* which I completed in the summer of 1990, and in which I dealt in rather more detail than was perhaps advisable with historic sites found along the river, beginning with St Peter's Church, Monkwearmouth, and ending with Witton Castle upstream in Weardale. In 1993 I decided to truncate and revise the accounts and include them in the present volume dealing with historic sites within the pre-1974 boundaries of County Durham.

My interest in County Durham's past dates from 1974 when I arrived in the North East with my parents and brothers after emigrating from Rhodesia. I was already keenly interested in history and coming as I did from a country where historic buildings were rare, was fascinated by the wide variety of historic sites located within the county. I still vividly recall seeing such places as Lumley Castle and Durham Cathedral for the first time, but my fondest memories are of Finchale Priory - which has to be one of the most beautifully situated monastic sites in Britain - beside which we lived in a caravan for much of the summer of 1974 whilst my parents looked for a house in Sunderland, my father's home town.

I wish to thank Andrew and Amanda Stephenson for accompanying me to many of the sites discussed and for their comments and encouragement. I am also indebted to my brothers, Shaun and Gavin Dodds, for taking many of the photographs which accompany the text. Furthermore, I wish to thank Ian Forbes of Killhope Lead Mining Centre and Paul Bidwell, Principal Keeper of Archaeology for Tyne and Wear Museums, for clarifying certain points.

Glen Lyndon Dodds
Sunderland, 8th August 1996

Map of
County Durham

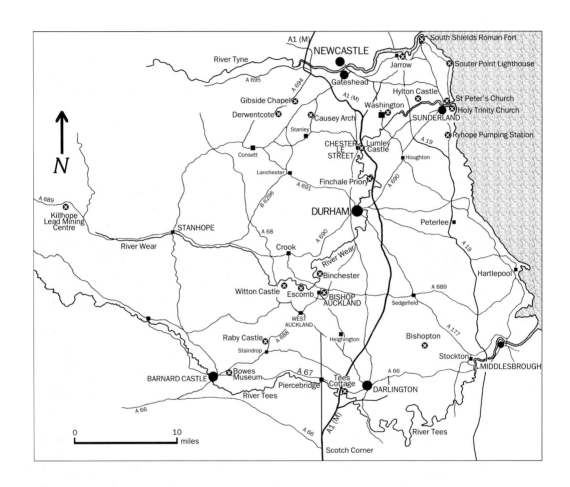

INTRODUCTION

ounty Durham has a rich historical heritage. Roman forts, imposing castles, a superb cathedral, and relics of the Industrial Revolution are just some of the many sites one can visit.

It is a heritage set in a land of contrasts. In the west are the windswept Pennine uplands where the river which flows through the heart of the county - the Wear - begins its journey to the North Sea. From its headwaters at an elevation of some 2,450ft above sea level it flows eastward down Weardale, before meandering northward just beyond Bishop Auckland through gently rolling countryside, the Wear Lowlands. It then heads east again, having long since cut its way through the East Durham Plateau, to reach the sea at Sunderland. Durham's fourth main landscape region, the Tees Lowlands, is situated in the south-east of the county and possesses good arable land.

Long before County Durham came into existence in the Middle Ages, people lived between the Tyne and the Tees. Small groups of hunter-gatherers existed here during the Mesolithic period or Middle Stone Age (c.8,000-c.4,000 B.C.). Flints and other objects testifying to their former presence have been found in the Hartlepool area and at a number of locations further up the coast. Material has also been found inland, most notably along the Wear between Durham City and Chester-le-Street, as well as in Weardale and the Gainford area next to the Tees. It has been plausibly suggested that the groups spent the winter months along the coast and moved inland during the spring or summer to catch fish, such as salmon and trout, which had swum upstream to spawn, and to hunt deer (and possibly aurochs) which had moved to their summer upland grazing territories.

The Neolithic period or New Stone Age (c.4,000-c.2,000 B.C.) witnessed population growth and the commencement, or at least expansion of farming, (which may have begun as the Mesolithic period drew to a close), with pastoralism evidently exceeding cultivation. Woodland clearance thus occurred on a fairly significant scale, especially on the East Durham Plateau, to make way for settlements, farming, and monuments such as the causewayed camp and cursus which cropmarks reveal as having existed at Hasting Hill, Sunderland.

The pollen record indicates that during the Bronze Age (c.2,000-c.700 B.C.) woodland clearance continued and that arable farming became increasingly important. Recent archaeological excavations at Carley Hill on the northern outskirts of Sunderland have indicated that alder trees were replaced during the 2nd millennium by cereal cultivation and that a large land allotment scheme existed. Until late in this millennium the climate was somewhat warmer and drier than it is today and allowed crops to be grown on the Pennine uplands. This was the case in Upper Teesdale and it has been reasonably suggested that a concentration of cairns above 1,000ft on Crawley Edge near Stanhope in Weardale, partly resulted from the clearance of stone from the land in order to render cultivation possible. Worsening climatic conditions towards the close of the period made arable farming at such altitudes impossible and probably resulted in an insecure society in which groups competed for productive land.

It might be supposed that bronze implements were common during this period. This was not the case. They were high status items and do not appear to have been as plentiful among the local elite as was the case in some other areas. It is thus ironic that one of the greatest hoards of Late Bronze Age material discovered in Britain was found in Heathery Burn Cave near Stanhope in the 19th century.

During the Neolithic era and the Bronze Age some of the dead were buried in or under burial mounds, and were often accompanied by grave goods. A number of burial mounds have been excavated in the county. One such, at Copt Hill, Houghton-le-Spring, was found to contain a Neolithic deposit consisting of several partly cremated skeletons. The disarticulated state of the remains suggests that the bodies had been left exposed to rot before being brought to their final resting place and set alight. The mound also contained a number of Bronze Age interments.

And what of burials from the subsequent Iron Age (c.700 B.C.-A.D.43)? As elsewhere in Britain, they are rare and one could thus conclude that the population must have declined. But such a conclusion would be erroneous, for other evidence indicates that Durham had a substantial population during this period, and it has therefore been proposed that the dead were generally cremated and the ashes scattered.

The Tees Lowlands are known to have been extensively exploited towards the close of the Iron Age, and evidence from elsewhere testifies that some other areas likewise witnessed significant activity. An interesting site dating from this period was excavated at Thorpe Thewles, about 2½ miles north-west of Stockton-on-Tees, in the early 1980s. Initially it consisted of a single enclosed farmstead, but in time it developed into a hamlet, with the enclosing bank and ditch being levelled to make way for this expansion. It appears, however, that single enclosed farmsteads were the norm and the presence of many such has been revealed by aerial photography. During the Iron Age many hillforts were constructed in Britain, but anyone interested in such monuments will find little to whet their appetite here for they are rare in the Tyne-Tees region. The most notable example is a multivallate site of 3.2 acres at Shackleton Beacon near Heighington.

Apparently Celts arrived in the region at some time during the Iron Age. What is certain is that when the Romans began subjugating the area in c.A.D. 70 the language spoken here was Celtic, as was the case elsewhere in Britain, and that at this date the region was part of Brigantia, the territory of a powerful tribe centred on Yorkshire.

The Romans remained in Britain for over 350 years and during this period many towns and cities were constructed - London was the largest with walls enclosing 330 acres - and much of the countryside became studded with villas, the country houses of wealthy officials and natives. However, the Tyne-Tees region was a frontier zone for most of the period, and though settlements developed next to forts which were established here, none was comparable to the fine towns found further south. Furthermore, the only definite villa known to have existed in the region was at Old Durham - near present day Durham City - and although its owners evidently had a comfortable lifestyle the villa was not particularly grand.

The majority of the known forts were situated along Dere Street, a Roman road which entered the region at Piercebridge (the site of a fort) and headed north past other forts at Binchester, Lanchester and Ebchester, en route to Hadrian's Wall (built in the 120s) and beyond. Some miles east of Dere Street ran another north-south road, now known as Cade Road, which entered the area at Middleton St George near Darlington and left it by crossing the Tyne at Gateshead. The only fort discovered along its length was at Chester-le-Street and was evidently founded c.175, later than the forts already mentioned, with the exception of that at Piercebridge which was founded in the 4th century: the latter probably replaced an earlier such installation. To the north of Chester-le-Street a branch road from Cade Road headed east to another fort at South Shields, which guarded a port at the mouth of the Tyne. There may have also been a fort at nearby Jarrow, and a number of signal stations appear to have been constructed along the coast.

2. Aerial view of Piercebridge from the north. The cropmarks show traces of a civilian settlement which adjoined the Roman fort located where the village now stands.

The lives of the natives seem to have been little affected by Roman rule. It is likely, though, that the Roman presence stimulated the economy with, for example, locals supplementing provisions and goods transported into the region for the army. It is interesting to note, for instance, that a recent analysis of grain discovered during excavations at South Shields has led to the conclusion that it may have been grown by local farmers.

Roman rule in Britain ended in or about 409, but it was not very long before other conquerors - the Anglo-Saxons or English - made their presence felt. Indeed, there is reason to believe that Anglo-Saxons had already settled in parts of southern and eastern Britain, having migrated from their continental homelands in northern Germany and adjacent areas with or without Roman encouragement. As the century progressed they were joined by many other Germanic immigrants (archaeological and other evidence supports the view of Germanic tradition that the number of settlers was considerable), and in the middle of the century relations between the settlers and the natives broke down. Prolonged conflict ensued, in which the warlike newcomers gained the ascendancy and spread west and north, no doubt engaging in a degree of 'ethnic cleansing' as they did so.

Several Germanic peoples were involved in the transformation of much of post-Roman Britain into Teutonic England, the most notable being the Angles and Saxons, with the former principally being involved in the conquest and settlement of the Midlands and the North. When did they arrive in the Tyne-Tees region? The earliest evidence for their arrival dates from the first quarter of the 6th century and it is apparent that Anglo-Saxon settlement north of the Tees was less intensive than in many other parts of the country. Nonetheless, some interesting finds have occurred. In 1982, for example, a pagan Anglian cemetery with the earliest graves datable to c.520, was discovered at Norton near Stockton-on-Tees, and some of the grave-goods indicate that the small farming community which used the cemetery maintained contacts with kinsfolk to the south for up to three generations.

At the beginning of the 7th century the Tyne-Tees region was part of the kingdom of a Germanic warlord called Aethelfrith, who proceeded to gain control of another Anglo-Saxon state, Deira, (in Yorkshire), and also extended his authority north and west by seizing Celtic territory. Hence the extensive kingdom of Northumbria was created, and during the rest of the century three of Aethelfrith's successors were the most powerful rulers in Britain. It was a time, moreover, in which Christianity became established in the North East (a bishopric was founded at Lindisfarne in 635), with a key figure in the Northumbrian church being St Cuthbert, a person of humble birth who ended his days as the much-loved and revered Bishop of Lindisfarne in 687.

By the close of the 7th century Northumbria's days of political dominance were over. On the other hand, it was beginning to enjoy a reputation for art and scholarship derived from work undertaken in monasteries founded during the course of the century. But this situation likewise did not last. A foretaste of what was to come occurred in the late 8th century when Viking raiders from Scandinavia appeared on the scene and wrought limited destruction. Then, during the 9th century, England was subjected to full-scale Viking invasions and these led to the end of monasticism in this region, a development paralleled in the country as a whole.

The 9th century also witnessed significant Danish settlement in much of eastern and northern England. Local dialects testify to this, as do many placenames. Most of the placenames of Scandinavian origin end with 'by' or 'thorpe', meaning 'village' and 'hamlet', and a glance at a map will show that such names are numerous in counties such as Lincolnshire and North Yorkshire. Scandinavian placenames are also found in County Durham, but they are not numerous and are mainly concentrated in the south of the county.

Scandinavian conquest and settlement in the South and West Midlands was prevented by Alfred the Great, one of the most attractive figures in English history, and during the 10th century his descendants extended their authority over territory held, or under the sway of, the Vikings. Thus the Tyne-Tees region was incorporated within the kingdom of England.

In 1066 England itself was invaded by William of Normandy. After his victory at Hastings he soon secured the crown, but further campaigning was required before he could truly regard himself as England's master. Indeed, it has been said that his son, William II (1087-1100), should really be regarded as 'the Conqueror' as far as this part of England is concerned. Certainly during William II's reign the North East was more securely in Norman hands than before, although the Norman settlement of the region through the creation of baronies and knights fees primarily occurred in the days of Henry I (1100-35).

In his pioneering study, *The County Palatine of Durham*, Gaillard Lapsley wrote as follows: 'During the middle ages...Durham was withdrawn from the ordinary administration of the kingdom...and governed by its Bishop with almost complete local independence.' The bishop was, for example, responsible for maintaining order: he appointed his own sheriffs and justices etc and writs were issued in his name from the Durham chancery. Moreover, among other privileges, was the right of full forest jurisdiction within Durham, a right which J. Linda Drury has persuasively argued dated from the reign of Henry I.

The palatinate had its basis in Anglo-Saxon times when kings granted gifts of land to the bishops from the foundation of the see at Lindisfarne in 635 onward. For instance, in about 883 a Christian Danish king who ruled from York granted Bishop Eardwulf and the 'Congregation of St Cuthbert' (i.e., the monastic community associated with his cult), all the land east of Dere Street between the Tyne and the Wear. Consequently, by the time the see was finally established at Durham in 995 - it was moved to the more secure setting of Durham owing to Viking raids - the bishops enjoyed extensive estates and rights of jurisdiction over those on these lands belonging to St Cuthbert's Church. In the generations which followed, the bishops' wealth, power and prestige, slowly increased. For example, in the 12th century Bishop Hugh du Puiset received mines in Weardale from King Stephen (1154) and acquired the overlordship of the wapentake of Sadberge - which included the majority of parishes on the north bank of the Tees - from Richard I in 1189. Durham thus developed into the greatest and longest lasting liberty held in private hands in England, and from the 13th century onward the bishops were said to enjoy within their franchise the same rights and privileges as the king enjoyed elsewhere: *Quicquid rex habet extra, episcopus habet intra.* Clearly, then, the regalian franchise's development was a gradual one which reached its height in the Plantagenet era. William the Conqueror did not, as is often stated, found the palatinate of Durham.

More than any other factor, the power of St Cuthbert's cult contributed to the special status of Durham's bishops. As Jean Scammell has commented: 'The root and repeated salvation of the Durham liberty were the extensive lands and ancient immunity of St Cuthbert: tribute to his enormous personal prestige, and to a shrine which was without rival north of East Anglia.' As noted, kings (and lesser individuals) sought to gain the saint's favour by giving gifts to his church. Moreover, they feared to incur his disfavour and thus, unless circumstances dictated otherwise, monarchs allowed the bishops a freer hand than was usual.

The majority of medieval Durham's population lived in the eastern half of the county, (there was nothing novel about this for the climate is drier, and the soils superior, to western Durham), and most were engaged in agriculture. Not surprisingly, the majority of boroughs were also located in eastern Durham. In all, there were eleven boroughs in the county. Most were founded in the 12th century - a flourishing period of town development in England - and the majority of them were established and controlled by the bishop. Two of the boroughs, Sunderland and Hartlepool, were located on the coast and the latter served as the principal port throughout the medieval period.

3. Seal of Bishop Antony Bek (1283-1311)

Occasionally during the Middle Ages, but particularly from the early 14th century onward, Durham suffered from Scottish incursions. However, the most serious visitation the county experienced was a natural one, the *magna pestilentia*, or Black Death. This arrived in 1349 and took a heavy toll. It was, for example, reported of West Thickley that 'no tenants come from this vill for they are all dead', while 78 per cent of the tenants at Jarrow perished. The latter township belonged to Durham Cathedral Priory and a study of the effect of the Black Death on the priory's 28 vills in the county by Richard Lomas has highlighted that the overall tenant death rate in these townships 'was slightly over 50%.' The plague made its mark in another way, by hastening the change from a society in which a predominantly unfree peasantry primarily held land in return for labour services, to one in which serfdom no longer remained and land was principally held in return for money rents.

In 1536, during the reign of Henry VIII, parliament passed the Act of Resumption by which the bishop's judicial powers were transferred to the king, and of the act Lapsley has commented that it resulted in 'the practical extinction of the palatinate.' Parliament soon passed another act which led to the commencement of the Dissolution of the Monasteries, whose wealth Henry's financially hard-pressed government wished to seize. The commencement of this policy was one factor which led to an abortive rising in Lincolnshire and the North, known as the Pilgrimage of Grace, a rising in which many men from Durham were involved.

In 1569, during the reign of Elizabeth I, another revolt occurred in which men from Durham, including the leading lay landowner, the Earl of Westmorland, participated. Its aim was to overthrow the Protestant queen and replace her with her Catholic cousin, Mary Queen of Scots, who was then a prisoner in England. But history repeated itself: the rising failed, and indeed was followed by more severe retribution than was the case in 1536, for over three hundred people in County Durham alone were executed.

In the early years of the 16th century Lord Dacre described Durham as 'an economic backwater, a savage and infertile country.' By the close of the century, however, it had entered a period of transformation in which its importance increased markedly. The coal trade was at the heart of this development. Coal had been mined in the county since at least the 13th century, particularly in the Whickham-Gateshead area, but during the course of the 16th century coalmining grew in importance because England was changing to a coal-burning society owing to a declining supply of wood. Sunderland, at the mouth of the River Wear, was one place which benefited. In 1565 it was described as 'in great decay of buildings and inhabitants', but in the closing decade of the century its stagnant economy was transformed by the establishment of salt works and by the exportation of coal brought downstream by keels.

In the 1640s England was torn apart by the Civil War and many men from Durham participated in the conflict though the county witnessed no major engagements. In 1646, following the defeat of Charles I, the victors abolished episcopacy. Hence the bishopric of Durham ceased to exist and this remained the case until the restoration of the monarchy in 1660. In the interval, Durham had sent MPs to parliament for the first time. It did so in 1654-56. Many in the county had been hankering after such representation for years but had been opposed by holders of the see who maintained that it was a privilege of the palatinate not to send members to parliament. Thus, following the restoration of the bishopric in 1660, the old ways returned and it was not until 1673, during a vacancy in the see, that the crown enfranchised Durham.

Economically, the 17th century also witnessed advancement. Coal exports continued increasing, while another industry, lead mining, entered a period of significant growth.

Lead had been mined in small quantities in the uplands of western Durham since at least the 12th century, but during the second half of the 17th century notable expansion occurred. Records, for instance, indicate that the majority of the veins on the bishop's estates in Weardale were being exploited in the 1660s. The boom in the industry evidently continued for the rest of the century until lead mining was adversely affected by the long War of the Spanish Succession, which harmed trade and industrial activity. During the course of the 18th century though, the industry revived and indeed rose to new levels of productivity. Among other industries which commenced or expanded during the 17th and 18th centuries were glassmaking, pottery and shipbuilding. Nonetheless, farming remained the principal source of employment in the county.

And what of religion? During the 17th and 18th centuries a wide variety of religious denominations was established and had devotees locally. Among such were Quakers, Baptists and Presbyterians. Methodism also took root. John Wesley visited the county on many occasions between 1743 and 1791 and at times encountered opposition, (at Barnard Castle in 1752 the fire engine was hauled out in an attempt to scatter the congregation), but Methodism flourished, as is attested, for example, by the number of chapels one can see in the dales.

4. Sunderland harbour c.1830, showing a collier putting to sea

As far as the economy is concerned, during the 19th century industry became supreme. Coalmining in particular dominated the life of the county, and throughout the century the Durham coalfield was the most important in Britain. Technological advancement enabled pits to be sunk through the magnesian limestone overlying the eastern half of the field (the first such was Hetton in 1822), and in all some 500 mines were sunk in Durham. Inevitably, pit villages proliferated, thereby more than doubling the total number of villages in the county. A government report of 1841 comments: 'Where formerly there was not a single hut or a shepherd, the lofty steam-engine chimneys of a colliery now send their volumes of smoke into the sky, and in the vicinity is a town called, as if by enchantment, into immediate existence.'

Railways were associated with the development of the coalfield. One such was the famous Stockton and Darlington Railway which opened in 1825. It was designed by George Stephenson and in addition to carrying passengers - it was the world's first public railway - carried coal to Stockton-on-Tees. Hence shipments of coal began for the first time from Teesside.

Shipbuilding also expanded notably. Sunderland was at the heart of this development, and in the mid 1850s William Fordyce aptly commented that the banks of the Wear were 'crowded with ship-building yards' and that Sunderland was 'emphatically the first shipbuilding port in the world.' Nonetheless, at this date more of Sunderland's workforce was engaged in seafaring than shipbuilding, which only became ascendant in the closing decades of the century and remained so well into the 20th century.

For most of the 19th century Sunderland was a boom town and its population grew dramatically, from 12,412 in 1801 to 146,077 by 1901. Immigration was the most important factor, with many of the migrants being from Ireland. Sunderland was the largest urban centre in the county but a number of other historic towns also witnessed significant growth. Darlington, a centre of the manufacture of linen, was one such. It likewise boomed, primarily owing to the opening of the Stockton and Darlington Railway which increased its trade and led to the establishment of locomotive engineering works.

Among the new communities which sprang up, the most remarkable growth occurred at West Hartlepool, one mile to the south-west of the ancient borough of Hartlepool which had declined into insignificance by the beginning of the 19th century. West Hartlepool was founded in the mid 1840s, primarily through the drive and ambition of an intelligent and enterprising character called Ralph Jackson, and expanded rapidly. Its first dock opened in 1847. Others soon followed, and by 1860 West Hartlepool was the most important port in the North East. Moreover, its growth contributed to the revival of its historic neighbour - which had witnessed an upturn in its fortunes in the 1830s - and in 1880 the docks of the two communities were joined to form one system, thereby creating an acreage exceeded only at London and Liverpool.

As Durham's economy was dominated by heavy industry it was one of the areas worst affected by the Depression of the 1930s. Mass unemployment occurred, with the most celebrated case being Jarrow, which had grown rapidly in the latter half of the 19th century after the founding of Palmer's shipyard in 1852. In 1932 the yard closed and in the following year Jarrow's unemployment reached 77.9 per cent. In an attempt to boost the region's economy, the government set up industrial estates, such as Team Valley Trading Estate (founded in 1938), to provide employment in light industry. It was, however, the Second World War which brought an end to mass unemployment. Paradoxically, for those in employment the inter-war years witnessed increasing prosperity. Wages fell, but prices fell further, and thus people's spending power increased and for the first time a wide variety of mass produced commodities were available for purchase.

During World War II County Durham was, for the first time, subjected to serious air raids. Sunderland was worst hit, for the Germans attempted to wreak havoc on its shipbuilding industry: 267 civilians were killed, over 1,000 injured, and extensive damage done to property.

The war seriously exacerbated Sunderland's longstanding housing problem. In 1936, despite measures to improve the situation, the town had been ranked along with three other places in County Durham - Gateshead, South Shields and West Hartlepool - as one of the five most overcrowded county boroughs in England and Wales. The post-war years thus witnessed a massive house building programme - growth was concentrated to the west of the town where 10,000 council houses were built between 1951 and 1959 - and comparable developments have occurred elsewhere in the county, though on a lesser scale. Furthermore, since the war three 'New Towns' have been created: Newton Aycliffe and Peterlee (founded in 1947) and Washington which dates from 1964.

Ten years after its foundation Washington New Town ceased to be part of County Durham, for in 1974 Durham lost its north-east and south-east areas, (Washington was situated in the former), to the new counties of Tyne and Wear and Cleveland. Although Durham gained part of the North Riding of Yorkshire during the boundary changes, its population was more than halved.

By this date Durham's principal heavy industries, shipbuilding and coalmining, were in decline. The former was affected by increasing competition from the Far East which resulted in over-capacity and hence the closure of yards due to lack of orders. The last yard to close, Sunderland's North East Shipbuilders Limited, did so in December 1989. The fate of the coal industry was comparable. In 1947, when the coal mines were nationalised, there were 127 pits in Durham, but a marked decline in their number began in the 1960s when demand for coal dropped significantly as other forms of fuel became increasingly popular. More than 50 per cent of Durham's pits closed in the 1960s and closures continued. By late 1993 Wearmouth, in the newly created City of Sunderland (the town was granted city status in 1992), was the sole survivor. But its days were also numbered, and on 10 December 1993 Wearmouth likewise closed, thus ending another centuries-old facet of life in the region.

On the positive side, some significant new industry has been attracted to the area. The most notable example is Nissan Motor Manufacturing (UK) Limited, which set up a factory at Sunderland in 1986. The car plant has proved a marked success. Indeed, on 1 February 1994, Nissan announced that it was Britain's principal car exporter after shipping 182,207 vehicles (84 per cent of its total output) to 36 world markets the previous year. Hopefully, success stories such as Nissan will attract more companies to invest in the area and help to ensure that the depressingly high rates of local unemployment, which have been consistently higher than the national average, will be reduced, thereby enhancing the quality of life for many inhabitants of a part of England with an interesting history and a vibrant historical heritage.

AUCKLAND CASTLE

A uckland Castle lies on the outskirts of Bishop Auckland and was once the favourite residence of the Bishops of Durham, largely because of its proximity to their principal hunting ground - Weardale Forest.

The first episcopal residence here is believed to have been founded by Bishop Hugh du Puiset (1153-95), an ardent builder and hunter. Additional construction occurred in the days of another notable bishop, Antony Bek (1283-1311). Though much of the previous structure was retained, the work was on such a scale that Robert de Graystanes declared that Bek 'constructed the manor-house of Auckland, with a chapel and chambers, in a most sumptuous way.'

One of Bek's successors, Bishop Bury, (1333-45) was a great lover of books and it is interesting to note that he completed a treatise extolling the value of such works while resident at Auckland. Bury said of himself: 'If I had been a lover of goblets of gold or silver, of high mettled steeds or sums of money, rich would have been my store. But in truth I loved books...manuscripts not florins, and preferred lean pamphlets to good-conditioned palfreys.'

Auckland Castle remained an episcopal residence until the reign of Charles I (who visited it on three occasions) when, following the Civil War of 1642-46, episcopacy was abolished and the castle was put up for sale by the victorious Parliamentarians. It was purchased by a leading member of their own ranks, Sir Arthur Hazlerigg, who proceeded to demolish its two ancient chapels and began constructing a mansion near the castle which he sadly neglected.

The Restoration of 1660 led to the return of the old order and John Cosin was appointed to the see of Durham. He demolished what Hazlerigg had constructed and began restoring the castle. Indeed, he exaggeratedly claimed to have 'rebuilt the castle of Auckland which was pulled down and ruined by Sir Arthur Haselrig.' He also reintroduced deer into the adjacent park.

In 1832 Auckland Castle's status changed, for it became the principal residence of the holders of the see - a role it has retained - when Bishop William van Mildert handed Durham Castle over to the newly founded University of Durham which he had helped to establish.

Description

Auckland Castle is situated in lovely parkland and was described in 1635 by a Cheshire gentleman, Sir William Brereton, as 'a stately and pleasant seat...of great strength' with 'a verye faire, neate hall as I have found in any bishopps palace in Engl[and].'

The castle lies to the north of a drive entered via an 18th century gatehouse at the east end of the marketplace, and is screened from the drive by a crenellated wall built in 1796 - the work of James Wyatt. The wall has a triple-arched and battlemented gateway, to the north of which is the entrance to the castle, again by Wyatt.

The porch opens to a narrow hall which is adjoined to the east by Cosin's Chapel, and to the west by what is now known as the Entrance Hall at the north end of a range extending southward towards the gateway. This range is in turn adjoined by one running west which is not open to visitors.

16

5. Auckland Castle from the south

The glory of Auckland Castle is Cosin's Chapel (formerly the medieval Great Hall), which he transformed into a place of worship in the 1660s, something which entailed heightening the building to form a clerestory. Henry Thorold has stated that entering it is 'breathtaking', while the late Sir Nikolaus Pevsner declared that 'Architecturally the interior of the former hall is the most beautiful work of the late C12 which the county possesses.'

The chapel is divided into a nave and aisles by impressive arcades. Each has four lavishly moulded pointed arches of grey Frosterley marble, and piers with two Frosterley marble shafts and two of light sandstone. The westernmost pair of piers have unusual waterleaf capitals, while the other capitals are moulded in a style characteristic of the 13th century. Cosin loved providing places of worship with splendid woodwork and the chapel was no exception. In fact, the stalls and screens are among the finest examples of his woodwork. They are of dark oak and have both Gothic and Baroque elements, with the latter predominating. In contrast, the attractive reredos dates from 1884 and is by Hodgson Fowler. The ceiling is also noteworthy. It has panels with geometric patterns and Cosin's coat of arms, and is further ornamented by motifs such as carved eagles and garlands. Bishop Cosin died in 1672 and was buried in the chapel on 29 April, and a large black marble slab in the centre of the floor covers the grave. His son-in-law, Samuel Davidson, had already been buried in the chapel while the bishop was in London: an occurrence which had led Cosin to declare that it was 'a sudden and rash act to suffer anyone to be buried there before myself.'

Stairs in the Entrance Hall lead to the state rooms on the first floor of the south range. Beyond an anteroom stands the Throne Room - both are in a block no doubt dating from the days of Bek - and the latter is lined with portraits of bishops, including work by Sir Thomas Lawrence, while at its far end is a throne set below a fine pinnacled plaster canopy and flanked by niches. A door in the south wall opens to the Long Dining Room in the middle part of the range, which dates from the days of Bishops Ruthall (1509-23) and Tunstall (1530-59). The room has both Palladian and Rococo decoration dating from the mid 1750s, and superb paintings of Jacob and his sons by Zurburan which date from 1640 and were acquired by Bishop Trevor, (1753-71). This room is in turn adjoined by the smaller and brighter King Charles Room - likewise in the Tudor part of the range - which was again provided with Palladian-Rococo decoration by Trevor. It is now a dining room. The southernmost part of the range dates from the late 18th century - it was begun by Trevor - and contains the bishop's private apartments.

Auckland Castle and park are open to the public and access to the latter - which contains an 18th century deercote - is free.

6. Cosin's Chapel

BARNARD CASTLE

'T he Castelle of Barnard stondith stately apon Tese.' So wrote the 16th century antiquary, John Leland. Barnard Castle is indeed magnificently situated for it is perched on an escarpment 80ft above the River Tees which flanks it to the west and south, and has commanding views up Teesdale to the north-west.

The castle was founded by Guy de Baliol, who hailed from Picardy. In 1095 William II granted him lands in the North East, including the substantial estate of Gainford in Teesdale which contained extensive moorland suitable for hunting and sheep rearing, as well as fine arable land further down the valley.

Guy decided to build himself a castle to secure his hold on the estate. Instead of erecting a fortress at Gainford he chose a site to the west at a point where the Tees was forded by an old Roman road, a site which gave ready access to the upland hunting grounds and the lowland farms. Here, at what was to become known as Barnard Castle, he constructed a modest timber fortress, apparently early in the 12th century. It was protected by a timber rampart which for most of its length ran along the top of a high bank of earth and clay, quarried from a ditch which served as a dry moat, and curved northward in an arc from the cliff overlooking the river to a no longer extant gully just above the castle. The stronghold was entered via a wooden gatehouse next to the south-west corner of the defences, and its principal building was a large wooden hall located along part of the western side of the courtyard.

Guy died in about 1125 and was succeeded by his nephew, Bernard de Baliol - after whom Barnard Castle is named - who initiated extensive alterations and additions to the fortress in about 1130. (Guy had already probably replaced the wooden gatehouse with one of stone). By the time of Bernard's death in 1154 a large stone castle was well in the making and was neighboured by a borough he had founded on the gently rising ground to the east. Work on the castle continued during the days of Bernard's sons, Guy, (who died before 1162), and Bernard de Baliol II who lived until 1199, and by c.1185 a splendid fortress, one of the finest in the North, stood majestically on the site and dominated the borough.

Inevitably, the lords of Barnard Castle played a part in political and military affairs. Bernard Baliol I is a case in point. For example, he fought at the Battle of the Standard near Northallerton in 1138 when an English army defeated an invading Scottish force led by David I who was eager to extend his authority south of the Tweed. Furthermore, Baliol took an interest in other matters. For instance, he granted land in Teesdale to a Yorkshire monastery, Rievaulx Abbey.

Another member of the line, Hugh de Baliol, who became head of the family in 1205 during the troubled reign of King John, incurred that king's displeasure with the result that Barnard Castle and his lands were taken into royal hands. By 1213, however, Hugh once again enjoyed their possession and he was to become one of John's leading supporters in the north of England. Consequently, in 1216, by which time England had descended into civil war, Barnard Castle was briefly besieged by John's northern enemies, chief of whom was Eustace de Vescy, lord of Alnwick, and during the proceedings Vescy was killed by a crossbow bolt fired by one of the garrison.

Hugh died in 1228 and was succeeded by his son, John, who rose to greater prominence than any of his forebears and was a loyal supporter of Henry III, whom he served administratively and militarily. For example, in 1264 he fought on his behalf at Lewes, the first major engagement of a civil war known as the Barons' War, and was taken prisoner by the victorious rebels.

John married Devorguilla, the heiress of a Scottish nobleman, Alan of Galloway, who had himself married a great granddaughter of David I. Baliol thus gained possession of extensive estates, in particular the Lordship of Galloway, and became one of the wealthiest men in Britain. To secure his hold on the Scottish estates he imprisoned Devorguilla's illegitimate half-brother, Thomas, in Barnard Castle in 1235 and he was still incarcerated when Baliol died in 1269 and remained such until 1296.

Evidently, Baliol's marriage to Devorguilla was a happy one, and following his death she displayed touching signs of devotion to his memory. For one thing, she had his heart embalmed and carried it with her in a casket until her own death. Moreover, in 1273 she bequeathed land near Dumfries to the Cistercians in order to found a monastery in his honour and, in 1282, gave Baliol College, Oxford, its foundation charter and early endowments thereby consolidating John's own provision of scholars at the university during his lifetime. Devorguilla died in 1290 and was buried, along with her late husband's heart, at the Cistercian monastery referred to, which thus came to be known as Sweetheart Abbey.

Following John Baliol's death in 1269 headship of the family passed in turn to three of his sons, the last of whom, also called John, succeeded in 1278. As a descendant of David I of Scotland through his mother, he subsequently became involved in the disputed succession to the Scottish throne which began in 1290. In 1292 Baliol, who enjoyed the support of Edward I of England who played a major role in the proceedings, was the successful claimant. However, the relationship between the two monarchs soon turned sour. Edward regarded himself as the feudal overlord of Scotland and thus treated Baliol as a vassal. Things came to a head in 1296 after Scotland allied itself with France, a nation with which England was at war. Edward invaded Scotland and overthrew Baliol who found himself incarcerated in the Tower of London. Later he was allowed to end his days on the Baliol's original estates in Picardy.

During the conflict in 1296 the Bishop of Durham, Antony Bek, a longstanding friend of Edward I, seized Barnard Castle and Baliol's lands in Durham, over which the Bishops of Durham had unsuccessfully claimed feudal lordship for generations. Bek visited Barnard Castle on a number of occasions and made some additions to its fabric. In time, however, he likewise fell foul of Edward I who seized the temporalities of the bishopric of Durham and the lordship of Barnard Castle in 1306. Though the temporalities were later restored, the lordship was granted to Guy de Beauchamp, Earl of Warwick, by Edward in 1307.

The lordship of Barnard Castle remained in the hands of the Beauchamps well into the 15th century. To the Baliols, Barnard Castle had been their principal residence, but to the Beauchamps it was peripheral. They were seldom in residence, and though they took a keen interest in the management of the estate, the castle was largely neglected, especially during the 15th century, and thus slowly decayed.

In 1449 the earldom of Warwick and the lordship of Barnard Castle passed to Richard Neville, (the son of the Earl of Salisbury), who had married Anne, the sister of the last of the Beauchamp line. Richard Neville is known to history as 'Warwick the Kingmaker', and was a central figure in the Wars of the Roses which occurred in the second half of the 15th century, although Barnard Castle appears to have not featured in the conflict. Perhaps its decline even continued.

7. Barnard Castle from the Tees

In 1471 Warwick was slain at Barnet and in due course the lordship of Barnard Castle passed to his son-in-law Richard Plantagenet, the younger brother of Edward IV, who was to emerge as the dominant figure in the North during the 1470s. Though Richard's favourite residence was Middleham Castle in Wensleydale, Yorkshire, he did take an interest in Barnard Castle to which he made some alterations. He was a deeply religious man and it appears that he planned to found an ecclesiastical college within the castle, though the idea never came to fruition. Richard was killed at the Battle of Bosworth in 1485 and Barnard Castle soon passed into the hands of the victor of that engagement, Henry VII.

In 1569 the incident for which Barnard Castle is best known occurred. This was a siege during the rebellion known as the Rising of the North which began in mid November. The revolt was supported by almost all the region's landowners including the two most powerful, the Earls of Northumberland and Westmorland, and its aim was to free Mary Queen of Scots, a Catholic, and the prisoner of her Protestant cousin, Queen Elizabeth, and place her on the English throne thereby restoring Catholicism. Initially the rebels bypassed Barnard Castle - which was held for Elizabeth by Sir George Bowes - for they headed south from Durham City into Yorkshire via Darlington. Instead of striking at the weak forces loyal to Elizabeth in Yorkshire, they frittered away time there before heading north and laying siege to Barnard Castle on 2 December with a force of about 5,000 men.

Bowes was determined to resist, but the same cannot be said of the garrison. On 14 December, after being forced to surrender two days earlier, he described conditions during the siege. There had been a 'great want of bread, drynck, and water; which was our only dryncke, save I myxed yt with some wyne. I fownde the people in the Castle in continuall mutenyes, seakyng not only, by greatt nombers, to leap the walls and run to the rebells, but also by all menes to betraye the [castle]...to the rebells. So far, as in one daye and nyght, two hundred and twenty six men leapyd over the walles, and opened the gaytes, and went to the enemy; off which nomber, thirty fyve broke their necks, legges, or armes in the leaping.' Even though the castle fell into the rebels' hands the eleven day siege enabled Elizabeth's lieutenants to gather their forces in strength and move against her opponents. The rising was as good as over.

In 1603 James I gave the lordship of Barnard Castle to his favourite, Robert Carr, Earl of Somerset, but following Somerset's downfall in 1615 it reverted into royal hands for some years until it became the possession of Henry Vane. In 1630 he began restoring Raby Castle, a few miles to the north, and commenced dismantling Barnard Castle to provide the requisite material. In 1952 one of Vane's descendants, Lord Barnard of Raby, placed the bulk of the ruined castle in the hands of the Minister of Works and between 1974 and 1982 a programme of excavations was undertaken which has illuminated aspects of its history and development.

Before discussing the surviving remains, it may be profitable to say something about the history of the castle's construction. As has been noted, initially Barnard Castle was a modest timber fortress protected by a stockade running for most of its length along the top of an earth bank. In c.1125, however, extensive alterations and additions commenced during the days of Bernard de Baliol I whose aim was to transform the original castle into the core or inner ward of a much larger fortress with three additional wards. The first phase of rebuilding continued until c.1140. The ditch was deepened - it was cut down into the bedrock - and a stone wall replaced the timber rampart. Moreover a small rectangular keep, perhaps of two storeys, was erected in the north-east angle of the castle, while in the south-west corner the stone gateway which Guy de Baliol had evidently added to his castle was converted into the three storey Headlam Tower. A new entrance was located in the curtain wall just to the east of this tower, and like the previous entrance, was reached by a wooden bridge across the ditch (which is now known as the Great Ditch).

In about 1140 work on the second phase of building, which involved erecting the defences and gates of the additional wards, began. Moreover, during this period some internal buildings such as the Chapel of St Margaret in the Outer Ward, and those known to have existed in the Town Ward, were also constructed.

Then, between c.1170-c.1185, extensive changes were made to the Inner Ward. The timber Great Hall, for instance, which was located along the west curtain wall, was replaced by one in stone. Among other changes were the replacement of the rectangular keep by a round tower (the most eye catching part of the castle), and the construction between it and the Great Hall of a Great Chamber whose alignment was north-west to south-east.

Following this work Barnard Castle experienced little change until the mid 14th century when Thomas Beauchamp, the son and successor of the Earl of Warwick to whom the lordship of Barnard Castle was granted by Edward I, reduced the castle's size and made it more comfortable. The manorial farm, located in the Outer Ward, was run down and the ward abandoned save for the Chapel of St Margaret. Furthermore, at least one of the buildings in the Town Ward was demolished. Hence the castle was largely reduced to the Middle and Inner wards. But here a very substantial building was erected in the Middle Ward, presumably to serve in lieu of structures lost in the Town and Outer Wards, which may have been used for stabling and brewing. Furthermore the defences were improved. Access to the Inner Ward in particular was rendered more difficult. The wooden bridge across the Great Ditch was replaced by one running along the inner edge of the west curtain wall, and on the north side of the ditch the approach to the entrance ran along the south front of the Headlam Tower. As has been noted, the entrance had been located just to the east of this tower (in the wall between the Middle and Inner Wards), but it was now located in a half-circular tower or demi-bastion built against the east side of the Headlam Tower, which projected southward to the edge of the Great Ditch. Additional work involved the construction of the Mortham Tower in the north-west angle of the Inner Ward and the rebuilding of the Great Hall.

Further work, intended to improve domestic comfort, was undertaken when Richard of Gloucester held the castle, though this was modest in scale. This included the oriel window in the Great Chamber and the enlargement of windows in the Round Tower.

Following Richard's death in 1485 Barnard Castle was almost entirely neglected until its purchase by Sir Henry Vane who, as noted above, hastened its descent into a ruinous state by using it as a source of building materials.

Description

The castle is entered via the North Gate. This opens to the large Town Ward, which appears to have always borne this name and likely served as a place of refuge for the townsfolk when trouble threatened. Among points of interest are the Dovecoat Tower (whose walls are covered in nesting boxes) and Brackenbury Tower. The latter, which is romantically linked with Richard III's Constable of the Tower of London, Sir Richard Brackenbury, solely because of its name, is of 12th century date. It is a two storey structure. The barrel-vaulted undercroft evidently served partly as a storeroom and partly as living quarters. On the upper floor was a comfortable, well-lit room. A loop on its east side, i.e., the curtain wall, was in time converted into a window complete with seats, which gave a view of the hustle and bustle of daily life in the town below.

8. The Inner Ward of Barnard Castle as it may have appeared in the late 14th century (Terry Ball)

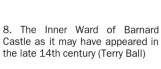

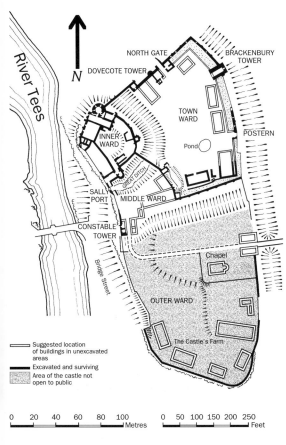

9. Plan of Barnard Castle

Suggested location
of buildings in unexcavated
areas

Excavated and surviving

Area of the castle not
open to public

Near the south-west corner of the Town Ward a modern wooden bridge (which rests on the foundations of a former drawbridge), gives access across a moat to the Middle Ward, the smallest of the castle's wards. The moat was dug in the 14th century and was originally filled with water and a dam on its north side prevented the water from entering the Great Ditch.

In the south-west corner of the Middle Ward can be seen the remains of the Constable Tower which appears to have been of three storeys and housed the gate from the Outer Ward to the south. The Outer Ward, the largest of the four, is not open to the public but fine views of it can be gained from the Middle Ward.

Between the Middle and Inner Wards is part of the Great Ditch dug in the 12th century, and it is crossed via a modern wooden bridge on the site of an earlier draw-bridge. On the north side of the bridge is what is left of the Headlam Tower. Only the west wall survives. A wooden walkway from this point heads east a few metres to the remains of the semicircular tower built in the mid 14th century through which the Inner Ward was entered.

An unexcavated range, said to have been three storeys high by 15th and 16th century documents, occupied the space between the Headlam Tower and the Mortham Tower in the north-west corner of the Inner Ward. It contained a number of apartments and the main kitchens. The west wall collapsed into the Tees in around 1800. The Mortham Tower itself, was five storeys in height, and though now very fragmentary is nonetheless fairly imposing. Most of its masonry dates from the 14th century.

To the north-east the Mortham Tower is adjoined by the Great Hall, which likewise dates from the 14th century and occupies the site of previous great halls. Little of the buttressed inner wall remains, but the outer wall still exists to roof

10. The Inner Ward as seen from the Middle Ward. In the foreground is the base of the demi-bastion

level. It has two windows (which appear to be set within recesses dating from the 12th century) and each window has two ogee-headed lights above which is an elongated quatrefoil.

Next to the Great Hall, and at right angles to it, are the remains of the Great Chamber, built in the late 12th century and later modified. The Great Chamber was the principal residential block of the castle and, together with the Round Tower adjoining it to the north-east, served as the private quarters of the lords of Barnard Castle. Its finest accommodation was located on the first floor - which was reached directly from the courtyard via a flight of stairs - and in the 15th century a fine oriel window associated with Richard III was inserted here in the west wall. It provides splendid views up Teesdale.

The Round Tower is the most imposing part of the castle, and is the northernmost part of the Inner Ward. A feature of its external appearance is the fine quality of its stonework. Internally its walls are honeycombed by mural stairs, passages and garderobes. The tower contained four principal chambers, all of which were circular and arranged vertically. That on the ground floor (which is the only extant room of the four), was poorly lit and housed a well. It was evidently intended to be used for storage, though the presence of a fireplace also suggests domestic use. Access to the next floor was via two flights of stairs, which also led to a doorway which gave access to the first floor of the Great Chamber. The room on the first floor of the Round Tower was its principal chamber. It had a large fireplace and a fine two-lighted window on its west side. The stairs by which the two other principal chambers above and the roof were reached, begin in the left jamb of the window. Both rooms were less elaborate, and this is especially true of that on the third floor which evidently had a military function.

From the east side of the Round Tower the curtain wall runs north-east to the North Gate, while another wall, to whose battlements the chamber on the third floor of the Round Tower had access via a flight of stairs, ran south-east from the Round Tower before curving south-west and, together with the Great Ditch before it, separated the Inner Ward from the Town and Middle Wards. Just over halfway along the wall (much of which has disappeared) are the remains of the Prison Tower, a projecting two storey addition of the late 12th century intended to strengthen the defences of the Inner Ward.

Its basement comprises an unadorned barrel-vaulted chamber, while the room above had a small fireplace and a garderobe. Within the Inner Ward, and close to the Prison Tower, one can see the remains of a square bakehouse which had two basic ovens.

Barnard Castle is cared for by English Heritage.

11. The Great Chamber and Round Tower

BINCHESTER ROMAN FORT

T he remains of Binchester Roman Fort stand a mile and a half north of Bishop Auckland on a spur of high ground overlooking a loop of the River Wear, which afforded protection on its south, west and north sides.

The fort was one of several founded during the Roman period in what is now County Durham, and like the majority of the others, was situated on the line of Dere Street, the principal Roman road which ran northward from York to Corbridge on Hadrian's Wall and into Scotland.

Binchester, known in Roman times as *Vinovia*, was founded early in the Roman occupation of the North for it was established by Julius Agricola soon after he became Governor of Britain in A.D. 78. He was no stranger to the province for he had served here as a young officer and had participated in crushing the Boudiccan revolt in A.D. 61. Moreover, he had returned to Britain in A.D. 70 to command the XX Legion and had subsequently led it on campaigns against the Brigantes conducted by Governor Petillius Cerealis.

The Brigantes were the most powerful people in the north of England and had initially been on friendly terms with the Romans. However, by A.D. 70 relations had soured and the Romans had decided to subjugate Brigantia. The Roman historian Tacitus, (Agricola's son-in-law), relates that Cerealis overran 'if not actually conquered the major part of their territory.' In c. A.D. 74 he was replaced by a governor who spent time campaigning in Wales and the task of completing the subjugation of the Brigantes thus remained when Agricola was appointed to the governorship.

An ambitious and able man, he was determined to do just that. After dealing with a hostile tribe in Wales, he moved against the Brigantes in the second year of his governorship and a timber fort may have been founded at Binchester at this time. If not, Agricola evidently established the fort in A.D. 80 when he advanced through Brigantia into the territory of tribes further north, including tribes living in Scotland.

Early in the 2nd century the fort was rebuilt in stone. It covered an area of 9 acres and was thus one of the largest founded between the Tees and the Tyne throughout the Roman period. Although evidently built by soldiers of the Sixth Legion, it was garrisoned by cavalry units composed of auxiliary troops, men raised from the provinces of the empire who served Rome without enjoying Roman citizenship. Some of the units which served at Binchester are known. At least one such was Germanic. This was the *Cuneus Frisiorum Vinoviensium* which garrisoned Binchester in the early 3rd century and was raised in Holland from among the Frisians.

Part of Binchester's function was to guard the point where Dere Street crossed the River Wear a short distance to the north-west. It also served as a base from which the surrounding countryside could be held and, following the building of Hadrian's Wall in the A.D. 120s, also served as an important supply depot for the Wall. Moreover, the fort was large enough to furnish accommodation for troops moving along Dere Street.

As with many other Roman forts, Binchester was associated with a civil settlement or *vicus* which developed outside it shortly after its foundation. The settlement became a large one. It covered 31 acres and was really a small town, and in addition to serving the needs of the garrison, functioned as a centre for native farmers, craftsmen and merchants.

The fort remained in continuous military use until the end of Roman rule in Britain in the early 5th century. After this it was evidently occupied by members of the native population, who also continued living in the settlement which virtually surrounded it. In time, Anglo-Saxons appeared on the scene and by the early 6th century parts of the buildings were being stripped or demolished and a section of the site served as a small pagan Anglo-Saxon cemetery. Further demolition work occurred in the 7th or 8th century when some of the fabric of the decaying fort was taken a couple of miles westward to Escomb where it was used in the construction of a church. By the Middle Ages the site was occupied by a hamlet, which passed out of existence by the 17th century.

That Binchester had an interesting past was, however, evident. In 1586, for instance, the historian William Camden had described the fort as 'well knowne to them that dwell thereabouts, both in reason of the heapes of rubbish, and the reliques of walls yet to be seene, as also for peeces of Romane Coine often digged up there, which they call Binchester penies.'

In the 19th century serious interest in the site began. The first excavations occurred in the 1870s under the direction of John Proud of Bishop Auckland and the Reverend R.E. Hooppell of Byers Green. Among other things, they excavated the remains of a large and well preserved bath house whose location had been chanced upon early in the century when a farm cart fell into a hole above the Roman hypocaust or underfloor heating system. Additional excavation was undertaken in the 1930s and 1950s by the University of Durham and the local archaeological society. Then, in 1976, a long term programme of excavation was commenced by Durham County Council.

Description

The fort was built to the standard military layout. It was thus rectangular in plan and had a defensive ditch behind which was a stone walled rampart 11ft 6in high, with corner and interval towers, and a defended gateway on each side. In the centre of the fort was the *principia* or headquarters building, and the *praetorium* or commandant's house, as well as workshops, granaries and perhaps a hospital nearby. Barrack blocks and stables would have occupied much of the rest of the fort.

Though the excavated remains open to the public only comprise a fraction of the fort's area, they are well worth seeing. They are situated near the centre of the fort and include a stretch of the *via principalis*, i.e., the main road, part of the commandant's house and his private bath-house, the best preserved Roman military baths in Britain.

One first comes to a walkway overlooking part of the *via principalis*. The road - which is actually part of Dere Street - ran through the middle of the fort, entering and exiting it through the south-east and north-west gates. The road is 16ft wide and its surface consists of river cobbles set in a clay and gravel base which originally would have been covered by small stones. Along its north side is a stone gutter while along the south side is a stone kerb.

Just to the south of the road, and likewise viewed from the walkway, are the remains of the bath-house's exercise yard and changing room The former was an open area covered with flagstones where someone intending to use the bath-house would exercise with weights and build up a sweat. An arch led into the changing room beyond. Here the individual would undress, put on a pair of wooden soled sandals, and enter the bath-house carrying a towel.

The bath-house, which is aligned parallel to Dere Street, is enclosed by a modern protective wooden building and is the most impressive feature of the site. It was constructed in about 350 for the use of the commandant, his family and guests. (Baths in the civil settlement served the garrison). The bath-house was enlarged towards the close of the 4th century and it has been suggested that it may have thus been used by more people, perhaps even the entire garrison.

The baths were similar to a modern sauna and were heated by an underfloor heating system supplied with hot air from two furnaces located outside the building. The air passed through arches into cavities under the floor before being drawn up hollow clay tiles behind the plastered walls to a series of chimney vents set in the roof. Hence heat was radiated by both the floor and walls.

The bather moved through three rooms. Time was first spent sitting on one of the wooden benches set against the walls in the Warm Room. This room had a temperature of around 35 degrees celsius and worked up a sweat again. From the modern walkway the original concrete floor can be seen. It is supported by a series of clay tile pillars.

Above floor level nothing remains of the room, which would have been about 13ft high and, like the other rooms, would have had an arched ceiling.

The bather then entered the Dry Hot Room. This was located next to one of the furnaces and was extremely hot. After sitting here for a while he may have received a massage from a slave. The room has not survived, but from the modern walkway fine views of its under-floor area can be gained. In the north-east corner two footprints in the concrete floor can be seen. They were made when the concrete was freshly laid and one is that of an adult, the other, that of a child. Steps lead down from the walkway to the under-floor area and here the bases for the pillars which supported the floor of the room can still be seen. Moreover, from here one has an excellent and unique view of an intact hypocaust - that beneath the Warm Room. A large arch through which hot air from the furnace outside entered the Dry Hot Room can also be seen.

Upon returning to the walkway one can see the remains of the hypocaust pillars which supported the floor of the Second Hot Room. This chamber was heated by another furnace (the massive side stones of an arched recess which led to it can still

12. The Warming Room. Beneath can be seen one of the pillars of the hypocaust.

13. The remains of the commandant's house

be seen), and was both hot and humid. Before making his way into the room the bather would have covered himself with aromatic oils. After entering, he would have scraped his skin with a curved bronze knife, thereby removing dirt and oil and helping to open up the pores. He would then have climbed into one of two hot baths and washed off any remaining dirt. Finally, he would retrace his steps through the bath-house and finish off by dipping into one of the cold plunge baths which adjoined the exercise yard.

Today, the Second Hot Room is vacated via a modern door on its south side. After doing so it is possible to view the remains of the furnaces before walking eastward to examine part of the commandant's house. This was a huge building, 148ft by 148ft, ranged around a central courtyard. Initially the site was occupied by wooden barrack blocks which were replaced with workshops in the early 2nd century supplying the garrison. The first commandant's house here was built in the mid 2nd century and was a half-timbered building with a suite of rooms (some of which had hypocausts), concrete floors and plastered walls. It was rebuilt twice and the last rebuilding evidently occurred around A.D. 340, i.e., some years before the bath-house was erected. Towards the end of the Roman period the rooms in the house were subdivided, possibly an indication that it was now used by a number of people other than just the commandant. For some time after the abandonment of the fort by its garrison, the house continued in use and the discovery of a large number of animal bones in one of the rooms indicates that it was partly used as a slaughter-house.

Binchester Roman Fort is cared for by Durham County Council.

BISHOPTON CASTLE

B ishopton Castle is situated in south-east County Durham five miles north-west of Stockton-on-Tees. The castle's existence was a short one. Nonetheless, Bishopton features in one of the most interesting events in the history of medieval Durham, an attempt to usurp the bishopric in the days of King Stephen (1135-54). Stephen's reign was marred by a vicious civil war between the king, who had succeeded his uncle Henry I, and Henry's daughter, Matilda, who believed that the throne should have passed to her. In some areas the prolonged war resulted in such suffering that the *Anglo-Saxon Chronicle* relates that people openly declared that 'Christ and his saints slept.' During this period, known as the Anarchy, unsavoury baronial characters built and garrisoned castles with what the *Chronicle* calls 'devils and evil men', and terrorised persons less powerful than themselves, in many cases intent on enhancing their own wealth and power rather than serving the cause of Stephen or Matilda.

Even allowing for exaggeration on the part of some contemporary sources, there can be no doubt that people did suffer greatly in many parts of the country and one of the areas which witnessed serious strife was the bishopric of Durham. The events in question occurred in 1141-44 and centred around an ambitious, able, unscrupulous and perhaps charismatic figure, William Cumin, the Chancellor of Scotland.

Cumin's origins are unknown, but he may have sprung from a family of clerks. He first appears as a member of the chancery of England where he worked under the tutelage of Geoffrey Rufus, who held the office of chancellor from 1123 until his elevation to the bishopric of Durham in 1133. Cumin, who had become a figure of importance in the chancery during Rufus' chancellorship, may have moved to Durham after his patron became bishop. What is certain is that by c.1136 he had entered the service of King David of Scotland - who modelled his administration on the Anglo-Norman pattern - and was indeed the king's chancellor.

David had designs on English territory, particularly the counties of Northumberland, Cumberland and Westmorland, and more than once during Stephen's reign he invaded England. The most notable invasion occurred in 1138 when he did so at the head of an army 'more barbarous than any race of pagans' according to Richard of Hexham. The invasion ended in failure when David was defeated at the Battle of the Standard near Northallerton in August 1138, and among those taken captive was Cumin who was thus briefly imprisoned. Despite the great victory won on his behalf, Stephen granted the earldom of Northumberland to David's heir, Henry, the following year. Some years before, in 1136, Stephen had granted David territory in Cumberland and so much of northern England was now either held, or under the sway of, the Scottish monarch.

In 1141 he was presented with an opportunity of extending his authority to include the Tyne-Tees region, the core of the bishopric of Durham, an area upon which he had already set his eye. The opportunity was presented to him by Cumin. In 1140, or early 1141, the chancellor was a guest at Durham of his old patron, Rufus, and upon seeing that Geoffrey's days were numbered he planned to seize the bishopric for himself upon the bishop's death. He won over a number of key figures to his side, including the keepers of Durham Castle, before hastening north to gain David's approval for his plan on the understanding that if Rufus died during his absence the death would be kept secret.

14. Bishopton Castle from the east

Rufus did indeed die during Cumin's absence, (on 6 May 1141) and for a while his death was concealed. Rumours, however, began circulating and thus after three days his body was handed over for burial as though he had just died. Cumin returned the following day, having gained David's approval. He took over the administration of the bishopric and secured support by making many promises. Among those who adhered to him were the majority of the barons of the diocese, some of whom, such as Robert de Bruce, held land in Scotland as well and no doubt gave their support to Cumin in part at least because he had David's backing. Crucially, however, Cumin failed to win over the Prior of Durham Cathedral Priory and one of the diocese's two archdeacons. He could not legally become bishop without a formal election by the chapter and pressure from himself and his supporters proved to no avail.

David likewise travelled south, and upon arriving in Durham formally placed the management of affairs in Cumin's hands and openly declared his support for the cause of his niece, Matilda, Stephen's rival. Though David threw his weight behind an attempt to have Cumin formally elected, and gained Matilda's backing, this did not occur: the prior and archdeacon remained defiant. David subsequently returned to Scotland and following his departure Cumin began to behave as though he were bishop. He compelled the citizens of Durham to take an oath of fealty and, with one exception, received the homage of all the barons of the diocese.

The exception was Roger de Conyers, one of the lesser barons of the bishopric, who had been enfeoffed with lands in southern Durham and Yorkshire for the service of three knights by Bishop Flambard (1099-1128). Conyers had been an influential figure in the administration of Rufus and appears to have been the constable of Durham Castle, and had been opposed to Cumin's attempt to become bishop from the outset.

Cumin's heavy handed behaviour cost him support, (even David distanced himself in 1142), and a period of military conflict began in 1143 in which Conyers was Cumin's principal protagonist. It did so after William de St Barbe, Dean of York, was formally elected Bishop of Durham. His election occurred after Prior Roger and Archdeacon Ranulph sent an embassy to the Pope to inform him about what had transpired and received a reply enjoining the election of a new bishop within forty days of the receipt of the mandate. Despite attempts by Cumin to thwart such an event taking place, de St Barbe was elected at York and consecrated on 20 June 1143 at Winchester. Cumin and his supporters were subsequently excommunicated.

Of events a contemporary source, the *Continuation of Symeon*, states: 'There arose a feud between Cumin and Roger de Conyers, from whom he could never extort either homage or fealty, as from the other barons. Roger, therefore, in self-defence, began to fortify his house at Bishopton for very fear of William. Cumin made an attempt with a strong force to surprise the place, [after 15 August 1143] but was repulsed and forced to retreat, and here the bishop found a safe residence....'

De St Barbe arrived at Bishopton after being invited to enter his diocese, no doubt by Conyers and a number of barons who had abandoned Cumin, and received their homage. Then, accompanied by Conyers and the other barons, he moved towards Durham, only to be driven back from Durham to Bishopton by Cumin's men who harried them all the way. At some time after 29 September de St Barbe moved towards Durham again. Intermittent conflict continued, but eventually the tide turned against Cumin - whose opponents now included the Earl of Northumberland - and as a result he surrendered to de St Barbe at Durham on 18 October 1144.

Bishopton remained the residence of the Conyers family for only a short time after these events, for they soon moved to Sockburn, a few miles away.

Description

Bishopton Castle was a substantial motte and bailey fortress. Its earthworks are situated on the south-eastern outskirts of Bishopton in what Robert Surtees described in the early 19th century as 'a narrow area of low plashy meadow, completely commanded by the rising ground... occupied by the village and church', and are clearly visible from the roadside.

The motte is 38ft high and its oval top measures 50ft from east to west by 30ft. The circumference of the base is about 200 yards. In 1990 Cleveland County Archaeology Section began a programme of works at Bishopton after being asked by English Heritage to devise a scheme which would restore the motte (concern had been caused by erosion) and prevent further deterioration of the gravel mound. A seeded covering of topsoil was thus placed on matting and the motte has been transformed into a well grassed mound with smooth slopes.

The motte is encircled by a deep circular ditch which is itself encircled by an earthen rampart. There is, moreover, an outlying ditch which is furthest from the motte on its north and south sides while a natural obstacle, Bishopton beck, runs just to the west of the site and would have rendered an approach from that direction difficult. Indeed, as John of Hexham commented in c.1160, the chief defensive feature of the castle was provided by nature for it was surrounded by marshland.

Bishopton is one of the finest motte and bailey castles in the north of England. It is, moreover, a fitting reminder of a brave and honourable man whose actions, when Cumin 'held by force the possessions of St Cuthbert desiring with blind ambition to be made bishop' (*Chronicle of Melrose*), were in marked contrast to those of many other men of rank at a time when the very word 'baron' is said to have been associated with villainy and selfishness.

BOWES MUSEUM

Bowes Museum is located on the eastern outskirts of Barnard Castle in southern Durham and is a splendid memorial to the cultured couple responsible for its foundation in the latter half of the 19th century - John and Josephine Bowes.

John and Josephine met in Paris, but while Josephine was of French birth, her husband hailed from County Durham. He was born in London on 19 June 1811, the illegitimate son of a Scottish peer, the tenth Earl of Strathmore, who owned Streatlam Castle three miles to the north-east of Barnard Castle, and a local girl, Mary Millner, one of the earl's former employees. John's parents had become lovers in 1809 and lived together at Streatlam, but in July 1820, just hours before his death, the earl married her in London in the hope that doing so would secure the title for their son, whom he had named as his heir some years before. However, the will was contested by the late earl's younger brother, Thomas, and the earldom thus passed to him. Nonetheless, young John Bowes was not left penniless, for the lands in Durham which had belonged to his father - some 40,000 acres with an annual rental of £20,000 - were allowed to him.

The tenth Earl of Strathmore had ensured that his young son received a good education, for when John was six he had sent him to a small private school run by the Reverend William Goodenough, who made a fine impression on him and with whom he remained on affectionate terms in subsequent years. In 1826 Bowes left the school and went to Eton, before enrolling at Trinity College, Cambridge, two years later.

He left Cambridge in 1832 and, as a gentleman of means, was persuaded to stand for election to parliament that year as a Whig, and thus in favour of parliamentary reform. He proved successful, and was to represent South Durham until 1847.

During these years he also devoted time to managing his estates. In 1840, for example, he sunk a pit at Marley Hill on his lands at Gibside in the north of County Durham. By such means Bowes increased his wealth. So much so that at the height of his fortunes in the early 1870s his income was £100,000 a year.

Bowes spent part of his fortune on art, something which had interested him from his youth. In fact he had acquired his first old master in 1830 while travelling on the continent. The journey in question may have been the first he made abroad, but it was most certainly not the last. Indeed, after coming of age he visited Paris almost every year (he became a member of the French Jockey Club in 1835), and was so fond of the city that in 1847 he decided to make it his main base.

John was also keenly interested in the theatre, and in 1847 he bought the Théâtre des Variétés, Montmatre, Paris. An actress of modest ability who worked there soon caught his eye - Josephine Coffin Chevallier. She was born in 1825, and was the daughter of a clockmaker. For a while John and Josephine lived together, but they then legalised their union by a civil marriage ceremony in Paris in 1852, and in 1854 underwent an Anglican marriage service in England to make the marriage valid here.

Meanwhile, the Théâtre des Variétés had proved a drain on Bowes' resources. Hence in 1855 he closed it and finally managed to sell the premises in 1858.

On the other hand, his marriage proved a blessing. The couple spent much of their time participating in the French social scene. But like her husband, Josephine was not a vacuous creature who cared for little other than partying. She shared, for example, his love of art. In fact she was a keen amateur painter who produced work of merit, being particularly fond of landscapes.

A source of sadness to the Bowes was the fact that they were childless, and it has been plausibly suggested that this may have contributed to their desire to found a museum which would be their own creation and serve as a lasting memorial. The idea of founding a museum seems to have taken root in, or about 1860, the year in which they decided to sell a chateau John had bought for Josephine in 1852 at Louveciennes near Paris as a wedding present. In 1862, by which time they had acquired a sizeable artistic collection, (which grew larger in subsequent years through the purchase of further material, including pottery, porcelain and tapestries), they managed to sell the chateau and proceeded to use the money to acquire land in Barnard Castle for the proposed foundation. In all, 20 acres were acquired between 1864 and 1870, and by the latter date construction work was underway, the foundation stone having been laid by Josephine on 27 November 1869.

The architect they had chosen to design the building was a Frenchman, Jules Pellechet, who had previously worked for the couple in France. Construction work was supervised by an Englishman, John Watson of Newcastle, who had built stables at Streatlam. He was authorized to change the plans in detail, which he did.

Josephine Bowes never had a strong constitution and by this date was frequently ill. Sadly, she did not live to see the museum project come to completion for she died in February 1874, leaving a grief-stricken husband, and a will and codicil containing detailed instructions relating to the foundation dealing with matters such as the appointment of staff and the museum's opening hours.

In 1877, by which time the shell of the museum had recently been completed, John Bowes remarried. The match did not prove a happy one. For one thing, his new wife, who

15. Bowes Museum under construction in the 1870s

was twenty-four years his junior, cared little for the museum which had become a major drain on his resources owing to declining revenue from coalmining. Moreover, Bowes became aware that his wife engaged in one or more adulterous relationships and in 1884 he commenced divorce proceedings. Bowes' marriage ended as his life was drawing to a close, for he died at Streatlam on 9 October 1885, leaving his estates to his second cousin the thirteenth Earl of Strathmore.

Work on preparing Bowes Museum for opening continued after John's death. In his will he had bequeathed £136,000 to the museum. However, it was not until 1900 that the trustees received the first payment of their legacy for Bowes' debts and sums bequeathed by him to a number of individuals had to be paid from his business interests first, and thus the trustees were forced to raise money for the museum by various methods.

Bowes Museum opened on 10 June 1892, and did so amid much ceremony and rejoicing. There was an enthusiastic response. Nearly 63,000 people visited the museum free of charge in its first year. Admission remained free until 1897 and became so again in 1905. Between 1898 and 1909 financial and building maintenance problems resulted in periodic closures and during both World Wars (when many troops were billeted in school buildings), the museum was used as a school.

Following the Second World War financial difficulties for the museum became acute. Inflation and maintenance work took their toll and so the Trustees sold items from the collection. Furthermore, admission fees were reintroduced in 1947. Then in 1949, the Friends of Bowes Museum, a society dedicated to supporting the museum, was founded with encouragement from Queen Elizabeth, whose father was the Earl of Strathmore. 1955 proved a year of crisis. The museum faced imminent closure and talks were held to try and safeguard its future. On 22 February 1956 Durham County Council - which had provided financial assistance for some years - agreed to take over responsibility for the museum, and the formal transfer of trusteeship took place in the presence of the Queen Mother on I November 1956. As Frank Atkinson has commented, 'thus began a fresh stage, an invigoration, in the life of the Museum.' For example, a number of specialists were added to the museum's previously undermanned staff and much needed decoration work was undertaken. Bowes Museum is still run by Durham County Council and Friends of Bowes Museum serve as volunteer guides for visitors to the museum which is open throughout the year with the exception of the Christmas period.

Description

E.Y. Western, a trustee of Bowes Museum, described it as 'Exceedingly handsome and grand.' It is indeed an eyecatching, and by British standards, very unusual building for as the late Sir Nikolaus Pevsner has commented, it is 'a sudden apparition...big, bold and incongruous, looking exactly like the town hall of a major provincial town in France.'

It is situated in well tended parkland and commands some splendid views. Upon entering the grounds two semicircular drives lead up to a terrace in front of the museum. To create the terrace a considerable amount of earth was removed in the space between the drives and the excavated area, as intended by the Bowes, was transformed into a formal garden though this only occurred between 1907-1913. The terrace enhances the impact of the museum which would still be imposing without such a visual support. The museum is 100 yards long, 100ft high, and crowned by three pavilions each of which, as Charles Hardy has commented, is 'big enough to contain a house of respectable size.'

Spaciousness is a major characteristic of the museum, and this is certainly true of the marbled entrance hall, the most sumptuous part of the museum. It measures 48ft 6in.

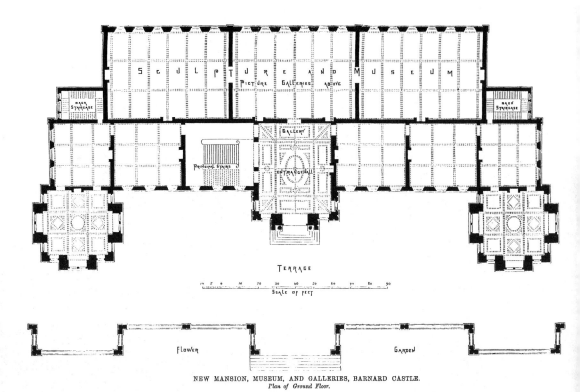

NEW MANSION, MUSEUM, AND GALLERIES, BARNARD CASTLE.
Plan of Ground Floor.

16. Ground plan of Bowes Museum

from east to west by 40ft and is 30ft high. On display here is one of the museum's most popular attractions, perhaps the most popular, the silver swan, a life-size automaton made in about 1773, which was purchased by John Bowes in 1872 for £200. Mark Twain saw the swan at the Paris Exhibition in 1867 and recorded that it 'had a living grace about his movements and a living intelligence in his eyes.' It is only operated once or twice a day to preserve it and its performances last for a minute. The entrance hall also contains life-size portraits of John and Josephine Bowes.

   To the east of the entrance hall, and still on the ground floor, are displays dealing with the history of the Bowes and the foundation of the museum, while to the west are displays illustrating aspects of life in Teesdale in the 18th and 19th centuries. At the back of the hall, a few steps lead to a lower level where rooms contain displays dealing with the fauna and flora of Teesdale and the archaeology of County Durham from the Mesolithic to the medieval period.

   From the entrance hall an impressive flight of stairs of polished granite gives access to the first floor. Here rooms contain a wealth of paintings, furniture and objet d'art, much of it French and dating from the 17th, 18th and 19th centuries, including items used by the Bowes while resident in France. One of the rooms is devoted to the Napoleonic period and contains an imposing portrait of the emperor by Girodet. Furthermore, several rooms contain English arts from the 16th to the 19th centuries.

   The second floor contains more specialised galleries. One room, for example, contains paintings by Josephine Bowes as well as personal mementos of both the museum's

17. The principal facade of Bowes Museum

founders. Other rooms display musical instruments, clothing, pottery and porcelain. There are, moreover, the museum's three main art galleries. The first gallery entered is the central one. This is devoted to Italian pictures and includes two large Canalettos purchased after a public appeal in 1982. The gallery to the west houses a collection of Spanish paintings, (one of the largest collections of Spanish paintings in Britain), and among such is El Greco's celebrated *The Tears of St Peter*. The easternmost gallery is devoted to Dutch, French and Flemish pictures.

Of Bowes Museum its present curator, Elizabeth Conran, has commented: 'The inspiration, for collection content, architectural style, and decentralised site, was French national museum provision, created after the 1789 Revolution. In every sense The Bowes Museum is a French museum in Britain....In scale and quality The Bowes Museum rivals the larger municipal museums. Yet it was conceived before most existed, and was built and filled by two people out of a private income. To make this vision substance was an act of great originality, skill and conviction.'

CAUSEY ARCH

I n the early 18th century, and for generations to come, the British coal industry was dominated by the North East. Some of the coal in the region lay beneath a thick layer of magnesian limestone and it was not until the first half of the 19th century that technological advances enabled this coal to be reached. Elsewhere, however, coal lay nearer the surface and is known to have been mined as early as the Middle Ages. Small-scale mining, for example, occurred on Tyneside in the 13th century where there were mines such as those of the Bishop of Durham at Gateshead and Whickham. During the 16th century the country moved towards a coal-burning economy owing to depleting woodland reserves and from this point on significant quantities of coal were shipped from the Tyne which dominated the coal trade until the early 19th century.

One of the areas which supplied coal shipped from the Tyne was around Tanfield in County Durham and here, in July 1725, a wooden waggonway - the Tanfield waggonway - came into operation to carry coal to staithes at Dunston.

Such a waggonway was not novel. The first such line is known to have been laid in Nottinghamshire in around 1600 by Huntingdon Beaumont, who was subsequently involved in bringing a 500 yard long waggonway into existence which carried coal to Blyth in Northumberland. The latter proved a short-lived affair, but other waggonways in the region soon followed (the earliest in Durham existed before the Civil War and was probably that known to have run from Whickham to Dunston), and by the early 18th century waggonways were a fairly common feature in the North East. However, the Tanfield waggonway was initially five miles long (it was later extended) and thus the longest so far constructed.

En route to the Tyne, the Tanfield waggonway crossed the Causey Burn via a bridge - Causey Arch - and recrossed it again about 350 yards downstream via a massive and still extant man-made embankment over a culvert: one of a number of embankments and cuts intended to ensure that the waggonway's route to the Tyne was as devoid of uphill gradients as possible.

Work on Causey Arch commenced in August 1725 at the instance of Colonel George Liddell and Edward Wortley, lessees of the Causey and Tanfield mines, and the bridge (which replaced a short-lived predecessor), was designed by a local stonemason, Ralph Wood. In June 1726, while building work was underway, the partnership responsible for its construction grew, for a number of other individuals involved in the region's coal-trade signed up and agreed to pay their share of the expenses. One such was a local coalowner, George Bowes, and from his accounts we learn that the cost of constructing Causey Arch was over £2,454, of which he paid over £731.

Several hundred waggons crossed Causey Arch daily in each direction, but it did not remain a scene of such bustling activity for long because between 1733 and 1738 the nearest pits closed, while in 1740 Tanfield Colliery went the same way after a fire. Nonetheless, Causey Arch continued in use on a reduced level for some decades to come - an engraving of the 1770s shows it still in service - but soon after this it fell into a state of disrepair. A print of c.1780 shows that considerable subsidence of the western approach embankment had occurred and by 1804 the approach had totally collapsed. Moreover, in 1812 the bridge itself was described as 'at present neglected and falling to ruins.'

18. Causey Arch

Though use of the Tanfield line recommenced in the 1830s Causey Arch was not restored. Instead the line was re-routed, for it would no doubt have been hazardous to entrust heavy steam-hauled traffic to the bridge, whose decline thus continued. Fortunately, though, recent restoration work (completed in 1981) has arrested this process and Causey Arch survives today as an important reminder of County Durham's role in the Industrial Revolution.

Description

Causey Arch is located in a scenic area which was described by William Hutchinson in 1778 as 'wooded, wild, and romantic'. It can be reached either by road or via the Tanfield Railway which carries steam trains conveying tourists between Sunniside and East Tanfield, stopping at Causey Arch en route.

Causey Arch is built of freestone, is 105ft long, and has a semi-elliptical arch which rises some 35ft from springing to crown. The deck, which is 10ft above the crown and about 80ft above the stream, is 22ft 7½in. wide and drained by hollowed stone spouts. Causey Arch was the largest single-span bridge in Britain and remained so until 1755. Neither Ralph Wood, nor anyone else in the world, had experience of constructing such a structure and so he relied on Roman technology.

The arch was crossed by two tracks of wooden rails with a gauge of 4ft. One track, the 'main way,' carried horse-drawn waggons heading to the Tyne laden with coal and in 1735 it was recorded that the waggons using the line were measured at 20 bolls, that is, they

19. A replica of an 18th century coal waggon at Causey Arch

each carried 44cwt of coal. On some stages of the journey gravity was the means of propulsion. The horse was drawn along behind the waggon and a hand-brake was used to ensure that the speed of descent was not too fast: on one quarter-mile stretch of the line the gradient was 1 in 12. The other track, the 'bye way,' was used by empty waggons on the return journey. The life-span of wooden rails was not long for they wore away easily. The 'bye way' thus lasted about three years while the 'main way' lasted barely a year. Consequently a double rail was used, and when the top rail was virtually worn away it was replaced without having to disturb the sleepers.

Of Causey Arch and the Tanfield waggonway, M.J.T. Lewis has aptly commented: 'We are so accustomed nowadays to the achievements of engineering that it takes some imagination to understand the contemporary astonishment at these works....In the 1720s nothing had been built on this scale since Roman times....Small wonder, then, that people came from far and wide to gaze open-mouthed at man's mastery over Nature in the cause of trade and industry....It might be said that it was on the Tanfield waggonway that British civil engineering on a grand scale first saw the light of day.'

DERWENTCOTE STEEL FURNACE

D erwentcote Steel Furnace is situated near Rowlands Gill in the valley of the River Derwent and dates from the early 18th century. It was probably built in the 1720s and may have been constructed by Denis Hayford who owned at least two other such furnaces in the Derwent Valley.

Derwentcote produced steel by the cementation process, which was first recorded at Nuremberg in 1601, came into use in England during the course of the 17th century, and was to dominate steel-making until the early 19th century after which it lost ground to cheaper and faster methods. Previously, iron bars had been repeatedly hammered and heated in contact with charcoal or coal, thereby converting the surface into steel. In contrast, the new procedure involved placing wrought iron bars and charcoal in stone or earthenware chests which were then subjected to prolonged heat in a furnace, during which carbon was absorbed by the iron which thus carburized and became steel.

In 1764 Gabriel Jars, a member of the Royal Academy of Sciences at Paris, visited England to observe industrial developments in the country and spent some of his time in the North East. While doing so he saw several steel-making furnaces in the vicinity of Newcastle and in his subsequent book, *Voyages Metallurgiques*, he relates how a man stood within the furnace and stacked layers of iron bars into chests, scattering slightly dampened charcoal between them. The chests were then sealed and a fire lit. Jars states that this normally occurred on a Monday evening, and that the fire was 'kept at the greatest possible heat until the following Saturday evening'. It then took a 'whole week...for the steel bars to become cold', whereupon the chests were emptied.

The steel produced by this method was known as 'blister steel', because when the bars were taken out of the chests they were covered in blisters where they had been penetrated by carbon. Derwentcote produced 12 batches of such steel a year, each weighing some 10-14 tons. Before blister steel could be used it had to be hot forged, that is, hammered at high temperatures, something which evened out the carbon content.

Derwentcote remained in operation until about 1870. Thereafter, it was used as accommodation by a local farmer for a number of years before falling into ruins following the Second World War. In 1985 it came into the care of English Heritage and restoration work commenced in 1987.

Description

Derwentcote is approached down a lane and lies on sloping ground falling towards the Derwent to the north, and is overlooked by trees. In contrast with most historic monuments it is unprepossessing. It chiefly consists of a long rectangular building consisting of rough blocks of stone of various size, roofed with red pantiles, and could be mistaken for a cottage were it not for a conical tower which rises from about two-thirds of the way along its length. This extends the full width of the building and is supported by buttresses internally and externally.

On either side of the tower is a room, each entered via an external door. The first room is the largest and contains a number of display boards. When Derwentcote was in operation it was partly used to store charcoal, coal, and wrought iron. Wrought iron was

20. Derwentcote Steel Furnace, viewed from the north-west

produced locally in a water-powered forge founded in c.1718 just to the north, beside the Derwent, which remained in operation until about 1880. However, in common with wrought iron produced elsewhere in Britain, this contained sulphur and phosphorus as impurities and so Derwentcote used high-grade wrought iron from Sweden which had been shipped to Newcastle.

Just next to the entrance, and close to the tower, is a door opening to a small projecting chamber which was probably a clerk's office. But unlike the other rooms - which afford views of the furnace - it is not open to visitors.

Within the base of the tower or furnace is a chamber containing two stone chests in which, as noted above, iron bars and charcoal were placed. When the chests were almost full they were sealed with a layer of sand and clay up to 8 inches thick. A fire fuelled by coal was then lit on a grate beneath the chests and had to be stoked roughly every three hours day and night for about a week. Flames and gases surged up a flue between the chests and rebounded from the chamber's domed roof down and around them, while side flues enabled some of the heat etc. to escape from either side of the chamber up the chimney. The furnace operated at a temperature of some 1,100 degrees celsius.

Derwentcote is the oldest and most complete authentic steel-making furnace to have survived in Britain, and is an important relic of the Industrial Revolution when the Derwent Valley was the centre of the British steel industry.

DURHAM CASTLE

T he Church was a dominant element in medieval society, so much so that some popes declared that they could even depose emperors. In England few men were more powerful than the Bishops of Durham in their heyday, for they held a unique position in the country being both prelates and lords of a great franchise - the palatinate of Durham - in which they enjoyed powers held elsewhere only by the king.

Though the bishops had a number of residences, Durham Castle was their principal one, a mighty fortress and a seat of government. The peninsula upon which the castle stands possessed communal fortifications in late Anglo-Saxon times, but the castle is of Norman origin and is generally believed to have been founded by William the Conqueror, of whom the 12th century historian Orderic Vitalis wrote, 'the king rode to all the remote parts of the kingdom and fortified strategic sites against enemy attacks.' William was undoubtedly aware of the importance of castles and thus it is evident that in 1072, upon returning from a military expedition to Scotland, he gave orders for the construction of a castle at Durham which would serve as a secure base for its lord, the Bishop of Durham, and his administration, and be a symbol of Norman power to the disgruntled native populace of the region who in 1069 had slaughtered the Norman Earl of Northumbria, Robert de Comines, and some 700 of his men shortly after their arrival at Durham.

The Bishop of Durham at the time work on the castle commenced was Walcher of Lorraine (who had been appointed to the bishopric in 1071), a learned character who was to play an important part in the revival of northern monasticism. Walcher's episcopate lasted until 1080, by which time the prelate had overseen the construction of a motte-and-bailey castle on the neck of the peninsula at Durham, with most of the buildings being constructed of stone. Among such was the east range (no longer extant), a building of some sophistication for it had high quality stonework and richly painted plaster, as excavations in the castle's courtyard have demonstrated.

The castle combined sophistication with strength. This was demonstrated in 1080 after Walcher and his retinue were murdered by an angry mob of Northumbrians at a meeting at Gateshead, some miles to the north-east. For upon slaughtering the prelate and those with him, the Northumbrians headed for Durham, intent on seizing the fortress, but were repulsed by its depleted garrison.

Walcher's successor, William of St Calais, was a highly eloquent and able man of whom an early 12th century work (evidently by Symeon of Durham), states that he was 'very conscientious in matters of divine and worldly business [and] had, moreover, such a keen understanding of matters that no-one could be found who could give sounder advice.' The bishop was a central figure in William the Conqueror's administration and it has been plausibly suggested that he was the guiding hand behind the famous survey known as *Domesday Book*.

In view of the above, most of Bishop William's time was spent away from Durham. Nonetheless, he is generally believed to have made some additions to the castle. For instance, he is usually credited with building what is known as the Norman Chapel, one of the most interesting parts of the surviving fabric.

Interestingly, St Calais' actions in the political arena led to Durham Castle being besieged once again, for in 1088, shortly after the accession of William II, the bishop became involved in a plot to oust the new king in favour of one of the monarch's brothers, Robert of Normandy. But things did not go as planned, and once the king had secured his position he sent an army north to bring St Calais to account. The force failed to storm the castle, and so on 8 September its commander, Philip of Poitou, made an agreement with the beleaguered prelate in which St Calais promised to face his accusers on condition that he had a safe-conduct to and from the royal court. In the event, after a reportedly dramatic trial at Old Sarum, St Calais was sentenced to the forfeiture of his fief (including Durham Castle) and went into temporary exile.

In 1099 another notable character was appointed to the bishopric of Durham - which had remained vacant since St Calais' death in 1096. The new bishop was Ranulf Flambard, and had gained notoriety in the service of William II, being the king's chief financial agent, ready and willing to resort to dubious methods in order to raise money. Following the accession of Henry I in 1100 - who promised to end the malpractices of the previous reign - Flambard was thus incarcerated in the Tower of London. Within months, though, he managed to escape, having intoxicated his gaolers, and during the summer of 1101 was restored to the bishopric of Durham following an amnesty.

Flambard's intelligence, good looks, stamina, strength of character and ambition, made him one of the most remarkable men of his generation, and although well thought of at Durham, his reputation nationally was for worldliness. William of Malmesbury, for example, relates that he had his monks dine on forbidden food served by attractive young women in figure-hugging clothing. Of the bishop's unsaintly reputation J.O. Prestwich comments: 'We cannot check the truth of all the stories told of Ranulf while bishop; but it is nevertheless significant that the stories were circulated as plausible and that they came from different quarters.'

Flambard made a number of alterations and additions to Durham Castle. For one thing, he extended its curtain wall southward so that it ran right around the peninsula, thereby enclosing an area of 58 acres within its defences. Furthermore, he demolished buildings between the cathedral and the castle proper so that, states a 12th century writer, the continuator of Symeon of Durham, 'the church might be neither polluted by filth nor endangered by fire.' Additionally, among other things, he evidently enclosed the wooden keep within a cylindrical stone wall, and built a hall along the north side of the courtyard and adjoining the west end of the Norman Chapel. In all, Ranulf was responsible for a massive building programme, of which Martin Leyland has recently observed: 'Flambard's sweeping changes and the end of his episcopate [in 1128] are a punctuation in the castle's development, a full stop. Thereafter changes took place within the scheme and design that Flambard had created.'

Within thirty years of Flambard's death considerable building work was undertaken by one of his successors, Hugh du Puiset, who was elected to the see in 1153. A tall and handsome man, Hugh looked, and was, an aristocrat, being the younger son of the Viscount of Chartres and the nephew of King Stephen. A fire in 1154 necessitated extensive restoration work, and much of the present fabric dates from this period. The fire began in the adjacent borough to the north of the castle, and according to an eyewitness, Reginald of Durham, spread to the fortress with the wind fanning the flames so that they 'rose up...more than the length of a lance above all the highest parts of the castle.' Severe damage was evidently done to Flambard's North Hall, while the west range (which appears to have dated from Walcher's episcopate) was completely gutted.

Durham Castle did not remain in Puiset's hands throughout his episcopate, for in 1173-74 he was the only English prelate who failed to support Henry II during a major rebellion and thus had to surrender the castle into the king's hands following the collapse of the rising. In subsequent years, however, he regained royal favour and the castle was in due course restored to him.

In the autumn of 1189, shortly after the accession of Richard the Lionheart, Hugh enhanced his importance by, among other things, purchasing the earldom of Northumberland from the monarch. (The earldom was confiscated in 1194 after Hugh insulted Scotland's king when the latter was a guest of King Richard). Furthermore, from November 1189 until March 1190 Hugh held the premier office of justiciar of England.

Hugh du Puiset died in 1195. Much has been written about this eloquent, intelligent, and at times tyrannical prelate. William Hutchinson, for instance, declared in the 18th century that 'Vanity was his predominant passion, and presided over all his actions. His ambition was unbounded, and his arrogance could brook no contradiction.' Many have viewed Puiset as a man of great ability and achievements. G.T. Lapsley was one such, believing that Hugh played a major part in founding the palatinate of Durham. However, G.V. Scammell has written an important reappraisal of the bishop's character and career in which he is generally portrayed as a man of humbler abilities and achievements. In the main this is convincing. Nevertheless, it would be wrong to become dismissive - a mistake not made by Scammell. It is significant that following Hugh's death some private charters both in England and Normandy (which he had visited on several

21. Seal of Bishop Hugh du Puiset (1153-95)

occasions) were dated: 'In the year in which Hugh, Bishop of Durham, entered the way of all flesh.' A quarrelsome nonentity with a penchant for publicity would not have made such a mark.

The next prelate who played a major part in transforming Durham Castle into what it is today was elected to the bishopric in 1283. His name was Antony Bek, and as with Puiset, he was of aristocratic birth.

Like previous Bishops of Durham, Bek quarrelled with his metropolitan, the Archbishop of York, for he consistently refused to obey the commands of his superior. Bek was moreover not averse to warfare. For example, he participated in Edward I's Scottish campaign of 1298 and at the Battle of Falkirk, where he tried to maintain discipline among his impetuous command, was told by one of his own knights: 'It is not for you, sir bishop, to teach us now of fighting, rather you should be busy at mass.' It was a remark which was as impertinent as it was unwarranted, for Bek was an experienced soldier and was described by another contemporary as 'the most valiant clerk in Christendom.'

The bishop's relations with his subordinates were certainly strained at times. Indeed, in 1302, following complaints made against him and his administration by disenchanted vassals, Edward I seized the palatinate of Durham and royal assizes were held at Durham with the result that many of Bek's officials were imprisoned. The palatinate was only restored to Bek the following year after he accepted a charter of liberties drawn up by the freemen of Durham. In 1305, however, the regalian franchise was confiscated again on grounds of maladministration following renewed complaints against Bek, with the Prior of Durham - with whom he had long been at loggerheads -being the chief complainant.

Bek died in 1311. He was undoubtedly one of the leading Englishmen of his generation. Some have viewed him as a ruthless and egotistical autocrat who gloried in his position. There is truth in this, but it is not the whole truth. There was more to Bek than this.

He was, for example, a very brave and able man who had a more convivial side to his nature than some have supposed, for he had the ability to win, and often retain, the friendship of others, and it is highly significant that he was the first bishop to be interred in Durham Cathedral. As C.M. Fraser has commented: 'Before his death Bek once more was lord of the bishopric of Durham and governor of his chapter, honoured, and at length nationally mourned.'

Two other prelates who left their mark on Durham Castle were Thomas Hatfield (1345-1381), and Richard Fox, (1494-1501). The former was a charitable and hospitable character who allowed Carmelite friars to preach in his diocese 'so that the souls of the people might be fed.' He was also a patron of architecture and an able diplomat and administrator. He was, for instance, heavily involved in diplomatic work concerning Anglo-Scottish relations. Indeed, Barrie Dobson has commented: 'It was for his many and various services in helping to secure his Scottish frontier that Edward III valued Thomas Hatfield most.' Bishop Fox was likewise a man of substance, and was aptly described by the Victorian historian, William Fordyce, as 'a man of high character, just, generous and able, but more of a statesman than a priest.'

Of one of Fox's successors a contemporary declared: 'He is justly considered as one of the most learned, prudent, and honest prelates in the whole kingdom.' Of whom was he speaking? Cuthbert Tunstall, who held the see from 1530 until 1559, during one of the most momentous periods in English history, and a period which witnessed the transference of the judicial powers of the bishopric to the king as a result of the Act of Resumption of 1536.

His predecessor, Cardinal Wolsey, had never visited the diocese and as a result Tunstall found 'the houses...belonging to the bishopric' in a dilapidated state, and did not have 'one house...to live dry in.' Thus, during his episcopate he carried out extensive restoration work, and in so doing made some notable additions to Durham Castle, including a fine chapel.

Of Tunstall, Lord Acton has commented: 'We may suspect that a want of...definite conviction had something to do with the moderation which is the mark of his career.' The bishop initially opposed Henry VIII's divorce proceedings against Anne Boleyn, but subsequently forsook her. He did a similar volte-face in regard to the Act of Supremacy of 1534, which made Henry the 'Supreme Head of the Church of England.' But while not 'quite the stuff of which martyrs are made,' (to quote an admirer, Charles Sturge), Tunstall did possess some fine attributes. He was a humane man, in marked contrast to a number of fellow churchmen, and it is worth noting that the distinguished Tudor scholar, A.F. Pollard, believed that Tunstall's long career was one of the most 'honourable in the sixteenth century.'

Another important figure in the history of Durham Castle, John Cosin, (1660-72), likewise found it in a state of disrepair following his appointment to the see. The previous bishop had abandoned the castle, never to return, in the face of an invading Scottish army in 1640. Then, following the Civil War of 1642-46, bishoprics had been abolished and the castle had been purchased by the Lord Mayor of London, but had nonetheless become increasingly dilapidated. Thus Cosin restored the castle, and did so with great verve.

As Percy Osmond has commented: 'In spite of his munificence, his unstinted hospitality, and his sociable bearing, Cosin was not a popular bishop.' This was so especially in regard to the gentry. In the main, they bitterly resented the way he thwarted their attempts to gain parliamentary representation. Cosin defended his stance by stating: 'All the counties of England send knights and burgesses to the Parliament, but the bishopric

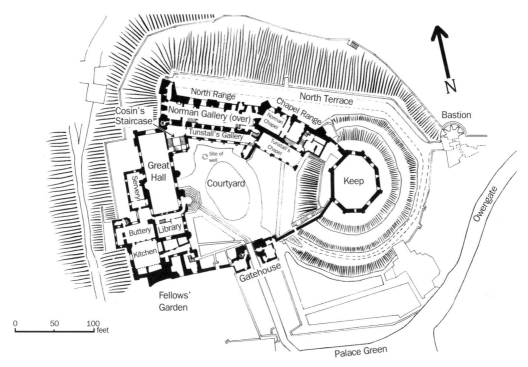

22. Plan of Durham Castle

and county palatinate of Durham sendeth none, for it hath by ancient custom and prescription, an immunity to the contrary, which the Bishop of Durham is bound by oath to preserve.' (The wind of change however, was such, that parliamentary representation was secured in 1673 following Cosin's death).

Durham Castle remained an episcopal residence until 1832 when Bishop van Mildert granted it to the newly established University of Durham which he had helped to found. Since this period Auckland Castle has served as the principal residence of the Bishops of Durham. Van Mildert was, incidentally, the last of the so-called 'prince-bishops' for some months after his death the remaining secular powers of the Bishops of Durham were vested in the Crown.

Description

Durham Castle is situated at the neck of a peninsula formed by a loop of the River Wear. Formerly, as noted earlier, its outer defences - which are now only partially extant - extended south and ran around the perimeter of the peninsula. The curtain wall in question was the work of Flambard (1099-1128), and according to a description written in the 1140s by a Durham monk called Laurence, was 'high and strong', being 'capped by lofty battlements with threatening towers at intervals.' The defences enclosed a large area divided by additional walls into inner, north and south baileys, and here, among other things, one found Durham Cathedral Priory and the residences of families such as the Hyltons and Conyers who had to perform castle-guard for their lord, the bishop.

The curtain wall had several gates. The most important was the Great North Gate, which Laurence states possessed 'parapets more stately than the others.' This impressive and formidable structure was situated at the junction of Saddler Street and Owengate in close proximity to the keep on its mound to the west, and was built in around 1100. It was extended into a barbican (c.1313), and then virtually rebuilt during the episcopate of Bishop Langley (1408-1436), at which time part of it was turned into a prison.

In its heyday the Great North Gate (which was demolished in 1820) controlled access from the adjacent borough, and it is interesting to note that in about 1315 the borough was itself provided with defensive walls to protect it against Scottish incursions, thereby indirectly giving additional protection to the castle. Some years before this, in 1303, Antony Bek's 'subjects' had been granted future free access through the Great North Gate, except in times of emergency or war, so that they could visit the shrine of St Cuthbert in Durham Cathedral - access the autocratic prelate had denied them.

Upon progressing through the gate, one entered the north bailey. From here the south bailey could be entered via another gate located at Bow Lane. On the other hand, upon heading westward up Owengate the inner bailey was reached after progressing through another gate in a wall running northwards from the east end of the cathedral to the keep. The inner bailey (today's Palace Green) occupied the space between the cathedral and the main buildings of the castle to the north. We are told that Flambard 'levelled' this area 'which had hitherto been occupied by...mean houses, and made it as plain as a field,' and it was here that the palatinate's principal administrative buildings, such as the chancery and law courts, were subsequently constructed.

Today the castle is entered via a gatehouse just off the north-west end of Palace Green. It consists of a tower with embattled parapets, buttresses crowned by battlemented turrets at each corner, and embattled projecting wings. It is disputed whether the gatehouse (which apparently replaced an earlier one probably located somewhat to the west), was built by Flambard or Puiset. The former seems more likely. What is certain is that it was partly rebuilt by Tunstall in the mid 16th century and extensively modernized by Bishop Barrington (1791-1826).

The approach to the gatehouse is a pleasant one, but it was once forbidding, for there was also an outer gatehouse linked to it by high battlemented walls, and a moat crossed by a drawbridge. The moat - which was very probably dry - appears to have been at least 57ft wide and over 19½ft deep. Cosin demolished the barbican in 1665, for it had fallen into a state of disrepair, and also filled in the moat.

North of the gatehouse is a courtyard and from here one can gain fine views of

23. Durham Castle's gateway as seen when approaching from Palace Green

24. The west range, taken from the courtyard

much of the castle. To one's left is the west range, whose appearance is enhanced by four polygonal buttresses crowned by cupolas, and an elegant portico with coupled Ionic columns which is approached by a flight of steps. The buttresses and portico were added by Cosin, who also constructed a tower which adjoins the west range at its north-east end. The tower has windows with a Tudor appearance in order to match those of Tunstall's staircase tower to the east, which projects southward from the Norman north range.

Cosin's tower adjoins the north range - whose windows acquired their Gothic appearance in the mid 18th century. Galleries run along the south front of the range from Cosin's tower to that of Tunstall, and are the work of the latter prelate. Indeed, the uppermost of the galleries is known as Tunstall's Gallery and gives access to Tunstall's Chapel, situated in the chapel range which adjoins the east side of the north range.

On a terraced mound further to the east, and connected to the east end of the chapel range by a wall of Norman date, stands the impressive keep. In plan it is an irregular octagon, with embattled angle buttresses rising higher than the rest of the battlements. Running down the mound - which is around 250ft in diameter at its base - is another wall dating from Norman times which runs from the keep to the gatehouse located to the south-west.

We shall begin exploring the interior by entering the west range. Though, as noted, the portico dates from the days of Cosin, the doorway was built during the episcopate of Bek and is badly weathered.

Upon entering, one arrives in the screens passage. This is the work of Bishop Fox and his emblem - a pelican piercing her breast in order to feed her young with blood - can be seen carved in stone here. To the south of the passage are four floors (not seen by the visitor) which contain a wine cellar, the library of University College, and residential accommodation.

The west end of the screens passage gives access to the buttery, a large half-timbered room which likewise dates from the time of Fox. This is adjoined to the south by the kitchen, which occupies a building likely built by Puiset, which was transformed into a kitchen by Fox in 1499. It is impressive, with three large fireplaces, fine brickwork - the earliest in Durham - and a roof of chestnut. There is, moreover, modern equipment because the meals of 300 members of University College are made here daily during the course of the academic year.

To the north of the screens passage is the Great Hall. It measures 101 ft from north to south by 35 ft, and is one of the finest castle halls in England. It has experienced a number of changes since its construction (upon a Norman undercroft), by Bek. Initially, it was about the same length as it is today, but was then extended south in the 14th century by Hatfield so that it became 131 ft long, but was then shortened to its present length by Fox. The Great Hall's timber roof is a survival from Hatfield's time (it was constructed by John Alverton) while two of Bek's windows remain. They are on the west side of the hall and are of two lights with geometrical tracery. The hall's most impressive window is at the north end and was inserted in the 19th century. It has stained glass by C.E. Kempe and commemorates the fiftieth anniversary of the university, and includes the arms of the university and of the bishopric of Durham.

In addition to serving its normal function - as a place for feasting etc - the Great Hall was also used for more weighty occasions. In 1494 it was recorded that a throne was located at both its upper and lower ends from which the bishop exercised his regalities when the hall was used as a setting for determining judicial matters.

An evocative description of the Great Hall was provided by the celebrated novelist, Sir Walter Scott, who dined here on 3 October 1827 when Bishop van Mildert entertained the Duke of Wellington. Scott recorded: 'We dined in the old baronial hall, impressive from its rude antiquity, and fortunately free from the plaster of former improvement, as I trust it will long be from the gingerbread taste of modern Gothicizers. The bright moon streaming in through the old Gothic windows contrasted strangely with the artificial lights within; spears, banners and armour were intermixed with the pictures of old bishops, and the whole had a singular mixture of baronial pomp with the grave and more chastened dignity of prelacy.'

Upon walking through a doorway at the north-east end of the Great Hall one arrives in the tower built by Cosin. This contains his famous Black Staircase, which is made of oak, but has balustrade panels of softwood which are pierced and richly carved in the form of foliage. Originally the staircase was simply supported by the outer walls with which it is bonded, but this proved inadequate and Tuscan columns were soon added to provide extra support. The staircase is one of the finest of its kind and period in England, though walking up it is rather disconcerting for the treads are not level, being lower towards the well than they are near the walls.

On the first floor landing double doors give access to Tunstall's Gallery, and towards the east end of the gallery is one of the most magnificent of all Norman doorways. It was built by Hugh du Puiset, and though now enclosed by the gallery, was originally approached directly from the courtyard via a stairway which evidently had a roof and open side arcades, as can be deduced from the weathering of the lower section of the doorway. The doorway has three orders of nook shafts with elaborately carved capitals, while the arch is semicircular and consists of three major orders separated by two orna-mented minor ones (the hoodmould above the outer order is not original). The major orders are also ornamented, principally as follows: the outermost by a series of deeply sunk and richly moulded octagonal panels; the middle order by richly moulded double

billets; and the innermost by square and rectangular moulded and sunk panels. The effect is truly
magnificent and moved J.R. Boyle to comment,
'nothing could exceed the richness of the mouldings of this doorway.'

Originally, the doorway served as the entrance
to what appears to have been Puiset's lower hall,
but this was subdivided by the time of Tunstall and
now contains a number of State Rooms seldom
shown to the public. The largest and most
imposing is the Bishop's Dining Room whose
Gothic appearance dates from the 1750s.

From the east end of Tunstall's Gallery one
enters Tunstall's Chapel, which was built in the
1540s and extended eastward to its present length
in the late 17th century by Bishops Cosin and
Crewe. The east window, though, was retained and
re-erected in the new east wall. Interestingly, the
extension looks older than the original half of the
chapel for its masonry, unlike the earlier work, is
not of ashlar. The oak stalls and stall ends date
from the episcopate of Thomas Ruthall (1509-23),
and were brought to Durham from Bishop Auckland by Tunstall. They are richly carved, and the
finest in the county dating from before the Reformation.

25. Hugh du Puiset's doorway

From Tunstall's Chapel visitors return to Cosin's
Black Staircase and ascend to the Norman Gallery,
which was formerly known as the Constable's Hall -
it was referred to as such from at least 1345 - situated on the upper floor of the north range. Bishop
Crewe (1674-1721) reduced the Norman Gallery's
width by installing servants' quarters along its
north side, and these were turned into rooms for
undergraduates during the 19th century. The
gallery has arcades along its west and south walls,
and of these the latter is the most impressive. It is
arranged in triplets, and the central arch of each
triplet is taller and wider than those flanking it and
opens to a Gothic window. All the arches are
enriched by chevron ornament.

At the south-east end of the Norman Gallery is
an original newel stair by means of which one can
descend to the Norman Chapel at ground floor level
in the chapel range. The chapel dates from the late
11th century and is the oldest surviving room in the
castle. Just when it was built is uncertain. Some
maintain that it dates from the episcopate of
Walcher, while others are of the opinion, and

26. The Norman Gallery

probably correctly so, that it was built by his successor, St Calais. Eric Cambridge, for instance, has recently argued in favour of the latter, and believes on stylistic grounds that St Calais probably used masons imported from either Maine or Normandy.

The chapel consists of a nave with north and south aisles. It is groin-vaulted, while the floor is covered in small rhomboid-shaped flagstones. The capitals of the six circular piers are sculptured, and the carvings greatly enhance the chapel's appearance. The most interesting scene depicts a hunter pursuing a deer and its young. The chapel was carefully restored in 1952, and is regularly used for religious observances.

And finally, what of the keep? It is not open to the public for it has little of historical interest. Laurence relates that in the mid 12th century it stood 'radiant with eminent beauty.' The keep of that time probably comprised a circular stone shell within which was a timber tower, taller than the shell, and connected to its battlements by a bridge. A contemporary, Reginald of Durham, tells us that at Puiset's accession in 1153 part of the keep functioned as a prison or dungeon. The bishop's principal accommodation may have been in the rest of the keep, though as Leyland argues it seems more probable that the bishop's quarters were located around the courtyard where, Laurence tells us, there were 'two great palaces', presumably the west and north ranges. In the 14th century Bishop Hatfield rebuilt the keep in stone for it had fallen into a ruinous state and the architect involved was probably John Lewyn, the most able English military architect of the late Middle Ages. In time the keep became dilapidated, and the present structure dates from 1839-40 when the keep was rebuilt by Anthony Salvin to provide residential accommodation for the university. It is faithful to the shape and ground plan of the earlier work.

27. The Norman Chapel

28. The keep

DURHAM CATHEDRAL

'**R**ising high above the surrounding river, which clasps it about in its protecting embrace, upon rocky, precipitous, and wooded banks, in near connection and combination with the neighbouring but not rivalling castle, it forms a picture scarcely to be excelled, and whose beauties no other scene can ever efface.' So wrote Canon Greenwell about Durham Cathedral in the late 19th century. The cathedral is indeed situated magnificently on a peninsula formed by a loop of the River Wear, and is undoubtedly one of the architectural wonders of the world.

Work on the cathedral commenced in 1093 during the episcopate of William of St Calais. When he was appointed to the bishopric of Durham in 1080 a Saxon structure, referred to in some sources as the 'White Church', existed on the peninsula and housed the shrine of St Cuthbert. The church was served by a non-monastic body, the Community of St Cuthbert. St Calais did away with both. First to go was the community. The bishop wished to found a Benedictine monastery at Durham and in 1083 he gave the secular clergy this option: they could either take monastic vows or depart. With one exception, they chose the latter, and so St Calais brought monks to Durham to form the nucleus of the monastic community instead.

Then, as noted above, in 1093 work on an imposing new cathedral began. It did so a year after St Calais had ordered the demolition of the Saxon church, which was evidently located just to the south of the site chosen for its replacement. This decision was in line with events elsewhere in England, for other Norman prelates had demolished the cathedrals of their predecessors and had begun replacing them with bigger and better ones of their own, grander indeed than those to be found in Normandy itself. It is sometimes said that the Saxon cathedral at Durham was entirely demolished before work on the new church began, but it is reasonable to assume that at least part of it was retained until services could be held in the Norman cathedral.

The identity of the master mason St Calais chose to design the cathedral is unknown. He may have been from Normandy, but if so it is apparent that he did not come to Durham directly from the duchy for certain features of the cathedral betray knowledge of buildings in England such as Winchester Cathedral.

By 1104 construction work, which as usual proceeded from east to west, was sufficiently advanced for the reportedly uncorrupt body of St Cuthbert (d. 687), to be translated to a magnificent shrine just behind the high altar.

When St Cuthbert's remains were moved to his shrine, most of the cathedral still had to be built. The great task was undertaken in subsequent decades, and by the time Geoffrey Rufus was appointed to the bishopric in 1133 the cathedral had to all intents and purposes just been completed. The task had been an enormous one. For instance, it has been estimated that approximately 68,190 tons of stone, quarried locally, would have been required during the construction programme. Though additions have been made to the cathedral, it is nonetheless essentially as built in Norman times, and is indeed the least altered Norman cathedral in England.

The cathedral was the spiritual heart of Durham Cathedral Priory, and life in the monastery naturally revolved around the observance of the seven Canonical hours which began at midnight with Matins and ended with Compline the following evening, before the cycle resumed again.

In addition to meeting in the cathedral for worship, the monks assembled in the chapter house at about 10 o' clock each morning. Here a chapter of the Benedictine Rule was read, sins openly confessed, monastic business dealt with, and saints and bene-factors commemorated.

Many of the monks also had duties to attend to. One such was the sacristan who was responsible, among other things, for ensuring that the cathedral was kept clean and illu-minated, and that bread and wine were provided for services. Study in the cloister was also undertaken by the monks where, moreover, novices - who were generally in their late teens and early twenties - received instruction so that, in some cases, they could progress through holy orders and become entitled to celebrate Mass. For some, such study proved onerous and frustrating. Reginald of Durham tells us that in the mid 12th century a member of the community called Robert of St Martin, a former knight, became so enraged by his inability to learn to read that he threw his psalter at St Cuthbert's tomb!

The main meal of the day commenced shortly before noon. When resident, the prior dined in his own lodgings where he entertained important guests. Dinner was thus supervised by the sub-prior, who sat at the high table, said grace, and kept a watchful eye on his fellows. The monks' daily fare usually comprised a loaf of bread, two portions of pulse or beans, two measures of ale, and two portions of flesh or fish each. But on feast days they had a more varied diet. The cellarer's list of provisions bought at Whitsuntide in 1347 for the community and its guests illustrates this point, for in addition to large quantities of meat and fish - 9 carcasses of oxen and 600 salted herrings, for example - he purchased 4 stones of cheese, butter and milk, 14 pounds of figs and raisins, as well as poultry, vinegar and honey, and spices such as pepper and cinnamon.

Over the years the monastery had many visitors, and we are told in a 16th century work, *The Rites of Durham*, that the reception and entertainment they received was not 'inferior to any place in England, both for the goodness of their diet, the sweet and dainty furniture of their lodgings, and generally all things necessary for travellers.'

Many of those who made their way to Durham over the centuries were pilgrims intent on visiting St Cuthbert's shrine, for St Cuthbert was the North's premier saint. The shrine was thus a source of great prestige and wealth for the monks, though it is interesting to note that St Cuthbert had a posthumous reputation for misogyny and women were therefore not allowed to approach his shrine. A marble line in the floor towards the west end of the nave marks the spot beyond which they were not allowed to pass.

Fugitives also made their way to Durham. They did so to obtain temporary sanctuary in the cathedral. After obtaining admission, they were required to confess the nature of their offence and were then provided with a black gown with a yellow cross of St Cuth-bert on the left shoulder. Sanctuary was provided for up to 37 days, and anyone who decided to leave England rather than stand trial was handed over to the authorities and transported to the coast after swearing a solemn oath never to return.

Overall, it appears that the standard of discipline maintained in the monastery was high. It is interesting to note, however, that a papal document of 1372 states that Durham's 56 resident monks enjoyed undertaking journeys in style, spending 'more on food and clothing' than befitted 'the modesty of their religion.' At times, moreover, we also hear of individual wrongdoers. One such was a monk 'gylty of the horrible synne of sodomye', who managed to escape from imprisonment during the priorate of John de Washington (1416-46).

Most visitors to Durham Cathedral probably envisage it in monastic times as a peaceful place, a haven far from the turmoil which at times marred life in the outside world. But strange as it may seem, at times Durham Cathedral Priory witnessed scenes of

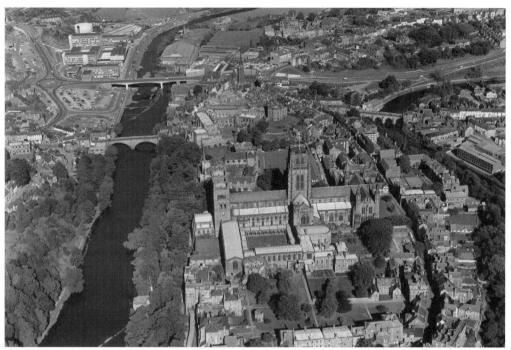

29. Durham Cathedral from the south

intimidation and outright violence. Indeed, on more than one occasion it was subjected to a siege.

Things most spectacularly came to a head in the early 14th century, with the principal protagonists being Bishop Antony Bek and Prior Richard Hoton, two tough and determined men. The former (who like other Bishops of Durham was the titular abbot of the monastery), received word from some monks that Hoton was behaving highhandedly. Hence on 20 May 1300, Bek, who was at least partly motivated by a desire to gain control of the priory, entered the cathedral with a retinue. Argument ensued in the chapter house when Hoton insisted that the bishop should undertake his visitation alone. Bek refused, and so Hoton walked out of the room, accompanied by his monks: excommunication by the bishop followed. Things went from bad to worse. Bek blockaded the priory and resorted to other measures such as cutting off its main water supply. Then, on 24 August, after the bishop's soldiers had forced their way into the priory, Hoton was dragged from the prior's stall in the cathedral and an appointee of Bek's installed as his replacement. Hoton proceeded to prosecute his case against Bek in parliament and at the papal court. The case dragged on for years, but on 1 December 1307 he obtained letters from the Pope instructing the Archbishop of Canterbury, among others, to secure the restoration of the priorate to him. However, he died before this could occur.

Monastic life at Durham ceased on 31 December 1539 during the Dissolution of the Monasteries, when the prior surrendered the house to royal commissioners. At this time the number of monks totalled 66 for the resident monks had been joined by others from the priory's recently dissolved cells, (dependent monastic houses), a figure comparable to the total number of monks for most of the priory's history.

During their visitation of the monastery the commissioners destroyed St Cuthbert's shrine, after which the saint's remains were moved to the vestry. In early 1542, on the instruction of Bishop Tunstall, they were interred in a grave specially dug below where the shrine had stood. By this date Durham had been reconstituted as one of the cathedrals of Reformation England, something which had happened on 12 May 1541. The last prior, Hugh Whitehead, was appointed the first dean, whilst the twelve prebendaries had likewise all been members of the monastic community.

In the first half of the 17th century one of Durham's prebendaries was a puritanical figure called Peter Smart, who gave a fiery sermon on 27 July 1628 in which he denounced the actions of fellow prebendaries at Durham, most notably John Cosin. Smart viewed the introduction of a more ceremonial form of worship at Durham as proof that Cosin and those associated with him were crypto-Catholics intent on undermining the effects of the Reformation. Among other things, he was angered by bowing to the altar and 'burning wax candles in excessive number when and where there is no use of lights, and that which is worst of all, gilding of angels and garnishing of images, and setting them aloft.' Smart's onslaught led to the loss of his prebendal stall which he only regained in 1641.

In the following year the English Civil War commenced and, as is well known, this led to the establishment of a republic following the execution of Charles I in 1649. It also led to the abolition of episcopacy and cathedral chapters by the victorious Puritans. Hence during the 1650s Durham Cathedral suffered from neglect. Worse still, it suffered from damage done by three thousand or so hapless Scottish prisoners incarcerated here until 1652 following Cromwell's victory at Dunbar in 1650.

Following the restoration of the monarchy in 1660, John Cosin and John Barwick were appointed to the restored see and deanery respectively. A programme of repairing and refurbishing the cathedral commenced and in 1663 - by which time Barwick had been succeeded by John Sudbury - the large sum of £4,306 3s 1d. had been spent and work still needed to be undertaken.

In 1777, during the episcopate of John Egerton, another important phase of restoration commenced for the fabric of the cathedral was in dire need of attention. The dean and chapter appointed a local man, John Wooler, as consultant while George Nicholson was the site architect. Among other things they rebuilt the north porch, and in order to cure the deep erosion of the cathedral's stonework, chipped away the surface to a depth of on average 2in. thereby flattening mouldings adorning the exterior.

As we have seen, from 1541 onward the Durham chapter comprised a dean and twelve prebendaries. In the 1830s, though, this changed during a programme of reorganizing the Church of England, and as a result the chapter came to comprise a dean and five canons, two of whom were professors in the newly established University of Durham. Today, one of the canons holds a professorship.

Description

The eminent architectural historian, the late Sir Nikolaus Pevsner, described Durham Cathedral as 'so overwhelming an apparition that no one will regret the time spent on obtaining the best general views of the whole building before studying its details.' The cathedral is undoubtedly magnificent, and its exterior is dominated by three towers, two at the west end and one - the tallest - above the crossing. The upper stages of the western towers are generally believed to date from the early 13th century (it has recently been stated that they may be late 12th century), while the crossing tower dates from the 15th century and replaced an earlier tower which had been struck by lightning.

The cathedral is normally entered via the main portal, located at the north-west end of

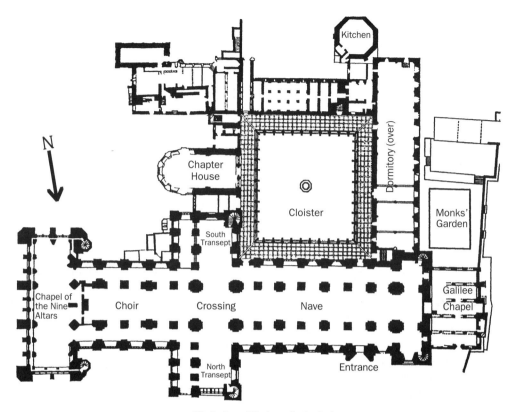

30. A plan of Durham Cathedral

the church, and affixed to its oaken door is a replica of Durham's famous 12th century Sanctuary Knocker which enabled fugitives to make their presence known and thus gain admittance.

Upon entering, one is confronted by the magnificence of the nave. This is of eight bays and is 201ft long, 39ft wide, nearly 73ft high, and flanked by aisles over 17ft wide. With the exception of the two westernmost pairs of arcade piers which are compound, the main piers are alternately compound and cylindrical, and on the inner face of the former are vaulting shafts which terminate below clerestory level in capitals from which spring the transverse arches of the rib-vault: diagonal ribs spring from corbels which are either next to the capitals of the vaulting shafts or above the cylindrical piers in the spandrels between the main gallery arches. Thus, in effect, every two bays form one major bay and this double bay system is found in many other Norman churches and derives from Jumiges (c.1040-67). At Durham, however, the intermediate supports - the cylindrical piers - are unusually imposing for they are 27ft high, nearly 8ft in diameter, and incised with chevron, lozenge and vertical fluting.

Durham's nave provides the visitor with a truly memorable architectural experience. Part of the impact derives from its size, but it is worth bearing in mind that some other Norman cathedrals such as Ely and Norwich have even larger naves. What makes Durham's so memorable is the great size of the cylindrical piers, the wealth of ornamentation on these columns and elsewhere, the high rib-vault with its pointed transverse arches (which date from c.1130 and are among the earliest in Europe), and the near perfect proportions of the elevation.

31. The nave, looking east down the cathedral

Before heading down the cathedral, it is best to first enter the Galilee Chapel which was built against the west end of the church in the 12th century by Bishop Hugh du Puiset. Indeed, at times the Galilee is the first part of the cathedral visitors enter.

The chapel is well-lit, though none of the windows is original, and was aptly described in the 12th century by the continuator of Symeon of Durham as 'a piece of most beautiful workmanship.' It is generally believed to date from the 1170s and is Transitional in style. It comprises five aisles separated by arcades, each of which has four semicircular arches supported by piers with waterleaf capitals. The arches are richly ornamented. Each has three rows of double chevron moulding separated by keeled rolls. The piers have four shafts each: two of Purbeck marble and two of sandstone. The latter have generally been viewed as additions dating from the episcopate of Thomas Langley (1406-37), but Richard Halsey has argued persuasively against this, maintaining that the sandstone shafts date from the days of Puiset.

Langley was certainly responsible for inserting the doorways by which the Galilee is entered from the nave aisles. The present roofs and timber ceilings are also his work. He also blocked the west portal of the cathedral by erecting an altar and his own tomb on the east side of the Galilee in front of what had been the exterior face of the doorway prior to the Galilee's construction. Langley's tomb has no effigy, and on its west side are three shields bearing his arms, while on either side of it steps lead up to the altar.

Langley's tomb is not the only one in the Galilee Chapel, for at the east end of the second aisle from the south is the simple tomb of Bede. His bones were brought to Durham from Jarrow in about 1022 by an enthusiastic and evidently unscrupulous collector of relics called Alfred Westou, and transferred from St Cuthbert's shrine to the Galilee in 1370. Bede's elaborate shrine here was destroyed during the Reformation.

Before leaving the Galilee, one should note the important survivals of medieval wall painting on the east wall. In the aisle to the north of the blocked central doorway, for example, one can see above 12th century work a scene of c.1300 portraying the Coronation of the Virgin set within a circular frame.

When heading eastward down the cathedral from the Galilee it is interesting to view mutilated monuments of the Neville family in two bays of the nave south aisle. One of the tombs is that of Ralph, second Lord Neville (d.1367) and his wife, Alice. Ralph was a distinguished soldier - the principal English commander at the Battle of Neville's Cross fought near Durham in 1346 - and the first layman accorded the honour of burial in the cathedral.

The Neville monuments are towards the east end of the nave and here, before progressing to the crossing, one can see evidence which shows that work on constructing the nave temporarily ceased not long after it had started. It did so after the easternmost double bay of the arcade, and one bay of the gallery, had been erected on both sides. Chevron ornament, for instance, is absent on the arches of the main arcade and the enclosing arches of the gallery, unlike elsewhere in the nave. Moreover, it is apparent that the nave was originally intended to have a wooden roof and that when work

32. The Galilee Chapel

recommenced it was decided to provide a rib-vault instead, in line with the rest of the cathedral. Hence Durham was probably the first church in Europe to be entirely rib-vaulted.

Since the 16th century progress from the nave to the crossing has been unhindered. But in the days of the monastery a rood screen - with sculpted panels depicting the Life and Passion of Christ - was located at the east end of the nave between the western crossing piers, 'in the body of ye church betwixt two of ye hiest pillors supportinge & holding vp ye west syde of ye Lanterne' states the *Rites of Durham*. Thomas Russo has plausibly suggested that the screen exceeded 13ft in height, and has aptly commented that as 'the liturgical focal point for lay services in the nave of the cathedral, the...screen and its attendant altar constituted an extremely important piece of ecclesiastic furniture'.

And what of the crossing tower, which as noted in the *Rites*, is partly supported by the easternmost piers of the nave arcades? It dates from the latter half of the 15th century when it was constructed to replace a less lofty tower which had been unsatisfactorily repaired after being struck by lightning in 1429. Prior Ebchester wrote of that tower in 1456, 'both in its masonry and timber [it] is so enfeebled and shaken, that doubts are entertained as to its standing for any length of time...whenever winds and storms are high, and we are standing at our duty in that part of the church, we tremble for our fate, having positive danger before our eyes.' The tower in question was hit by lightning again in 1459, and so between the mid 1460s and the late 1480s the present crossing tower was constructed. The lantern is 155ft high internally and as Pevsner has commented, the 'wonderful thing about [it] is the suddenness with which its quite un-Norman height meets the eye, after one has felt, in Norman terms, the nave itself to be so splendidly high.'

As for the transepts, both are of course rib-vaulted, with the transverse arches being semicircular, unlike those in the nave. Whether vaults were an integral part of the plan for the transepts is strongly contested. What is beyond doubt is that the vaulting in the north transept is some years earlier than that of the south transept. It dates from about 1110 and in contrast to the corresponding vault, is devoid of chevron ornament.

Both transepts have an east aisle. The arcade piers here, like those in the nave, are either compound or cylindrical and the latter, with the exception of the southernmost column in the south transept, are ornamented with spiral grooves. The exception has zig-zag grooving, and it has been plausibly suggested that this was probably the first time that chevron ornament - the favourite Norman motif of the 12th century - was used on such a grand scale anywhere.

The south transept contains Prior Castell's clock which was erected in the early years of the 16th century, renovated by Dean Hunt in 1630, removed in the 1840s, and re-erected in 1938. It stands on marble shafts, is surmounted by a lofty finial, and is very ornate. Nearby is a doorway which gives access to the stairs of the crossing tower, and upon ascending these panoramic views of Durham City and much of the surrounding countryside can be enjoyed.

33. Hatfield's tomb and the bishop's throne

And so to the oldest part of the cathedral - the choir - which is entered via a triple-arched marble screen. The screen is by Sir George Gilbert Scott and only dates from the 1870s, though one would have been here in monastic times.

The choir is 132ft long and has a superb marble floor - again by Scott. It is, moreover, richly furnished. The dark stalls, for instance, date from about 1665, i.e., the episcopate of Cosin, who was fond of adorning places of worship with superb woodwork, and are lavishly carved.

East of the stalls, and on the south side of the choir, is the tomb of Bishop Hatfield (d.1381), with an alabaster effigy. It is situated beneath an imposing platform erected during Hatfield's pontificate and upon which is the episcopal throne, reputedly the highest in Christendom.

At the east end of the choir, behind the high altar, is the highly attractive and important Neville Screen of c.1380 which originally had 107 alabaster figures. It is of Caen stone and was made in London - possibly by the notable Henry Yevele - and was shipped to Newcastle and assembled at Durham. It was largely paid for by John, Lord Neville of Raby, one of the Nevilles entombed in the nave.

34. The easternmost bays of the choir, with both Norman and Early English work.

The arcade piers of the choir are again alternately compound and cylindrical, and the latter are ornamented with spiral grooves. This is almost certainly the first instance of the motif being incised in stone on such a scale, and it has been reasonably suggested that the spiral piers are a deliberate iconographic reference to the spiral columns of the former shrine of St Peter in Old St Peter's, Rome.

Furthermore, the choir is rib-vaulted. Here, however, unlike in the nave and transepts, transverse arches not only spring from the compound piers but also do so from above the cylindrical supports. The present vault dates from the mid 13th century and replaced the original one, which is generally considered to have been the first high rib-vault in Europe and by then was 'full of fissures and cracks' at its east end. It might thus be supposed that in Norman times there were no transversals springing from above the cylindrical piers, but a recent examination has shown that they were a feature of the Romanesque vault.

Immediately behind the Neville Screen is the feretory, reached by stairs from both aisles of the choir. Here one finds the grave of St Cuthbert, which is marked by a simple slab in the floor. Interestingly, shallow depressions in the pavement beside the grave have been attributed, and no doubt correctly, to the scuffing of toes of people who knelt by the shrine to pray. Here too, just to the east of the grave, lead inserted into the stone floor marks the position of the main apse - one of three - which originally formed the east end of the cathedral.

Before progressing eastward to the Chapel of the Nine Altars, it should be noted that the choir aisles (in common with those of the nave and transepts) are ornamented by blind arcades with intersecting arches, an early appearance of this motif, and have their original rib-vaults.

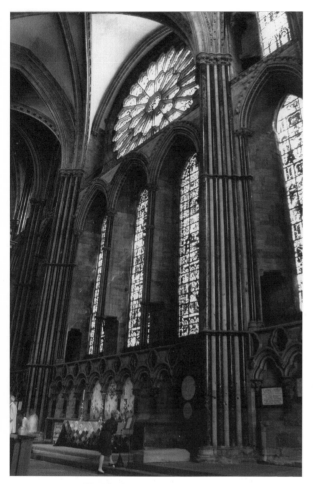

35. The Chapel of the Nine Altars

In the 1230s it was decided to replace the apsidal east end of the church with the present transeptal Chapel of the Nine Altars. Construction of the chapel commenced in 1242 and continued for some forty years, and entailed the rebuilding of the easternmost bay of the choir.

While the choir is partly Gothic in style, the Nine Altars is pure Gothic: a splendid example of mature Early English architecture. It was modelled on the Chapel of the Nine Altars at Fountains Abbey in Yorkshire and was probably primarily intended to enhance the setting of St Cuthbert's shrine and to provide ample space around it for pilgrims.

The chapel is 131 ft long by 38ft and its floor level is 2ft 8in. below that of the choir aisles from which it is entered, something which contributes to its impressive verticality. It comprises three main bays (the central one is the same width as the choir,) and the outer bays are each divided into three lesser ones by vaulting piers. On the east side of the chapel each of these piers has five Frosterley marble shafts alternating with four stone ones, and has stiff-leaf capitals, while the vaulting piers flanking the central bay are more impressive, for they both have seven Frosterley marble shafts alternating with six stone ones and again have stiff-leaf capitals.

With the exception of the north wall, the walls are divided horizontally into two main stages, and all the walls have arcades which are more elaborate than the blank arcades one finds elsewhere in the cathedral. They have, for instance, marble shafts with stiff-leaf capitals, and headstops in the spandrels.

The chapel has many lancet windows. There are eight and fifteen in the south and east walls respectively. Moreover, in the upper stage of the central bay, and thus above three of the lancets in the east wall, is a large rose window with thirty-six trefoiled lights radiating from a central light. It is the work of James Wyatt, (1795), though a round window has no doubt always existed here. The north wall contains the massive and magnificent Joseph window, which dates from the 1280s and is one of the finest 13th century windows in England. It is of six-lights, and has double tracery comprising intersecting bars and eleven foiled circles: eight trefoiled and three cinquefoiled.

The chapel is vaulted throughout at the same level as the choir, and the most impressive vault is that of the central bay. It has eight ribs, which spring in slightly diverging pairs from the piers on either side of the chapel, and in the centre of the vault they enclose a large ring which has superbly carved figures.

Finally, on the north side of the chapel is a statue of Bishop William van Mildert (d.1836), the last of Durham's so-called 'prince-bishops,' while just in front of this attractive work is the grave of the renowned Antony Bek who died in 1311. It is marked by a large slab of Frosterley marble.

Upon retracing one's steps down the cathedral one enters the cloister via doorways at the east and west ends of the nave south aisle. The cloister is surrounded by the former monastic ranges, but these are unfortunately mostly not open to the public. Among the rooms thus not seen are the chapter house in the middle of the east range, an impressive room completed between 1133-41, (though its apsidal east end was rebuilt in 1895), and the monks' kitchen off the south-west end of the south range. The latter, which was designed by the celebrated architect John Lewyn, dates from 1366-74 and has a remarkable vault with intersecting ribs which form a perfect eight-cornered star. On the other hand, visitors are often able to see the Monks' Dormitory, located on the upper floor of the west range. It was built between 1398-1404 as a replacement for an earlier dormitory and is 194ft long by 39ft. It has its original timber roof and tall two-light Perpendicular windows and, among other things, houses an important collection of Anglo-Saxon sculpture. In the undercroft beneath the centre of the dormitory, is the treasury where many other interesting objects can also be seen, including St Cuthbert's coffin and relief panels which belonged to the Romanesque rood screen.

The 12th century historian, William of Malmesbury, said of the Normans that 'they wished to have huge buildings' and when one visits great Norman cathedrals such as Durham it is immediately apparent that they transformed this wish into reality. But Durham is more than just a massive building. It is an architectural tour de force, justly famed for its precocious use of the rib-vault (at the very least, an aesthetic improvement on groin- and barrel-vaults), and its wealth of ornamentation - which is probably partly due to inspiration provided by the Anglo-Saxon fondness for surface enrichment - and one of the principal differences between Durham and earlier Norman cathedrals such as Winchester. The latter, for instance, has arcades with cylindrical piers alternating with compound ones, but its cylindrical piers are plain, as are the arches, while at Durham they are respectively incised with decoration and moulded. As Geoffrey Webb has said of Durham: 'Both in the management of the proportions and the disposition of the ornament, there is an impression of mastery that distinguishes it from all its near contemporaries.' It was a point not lost on others. The cathedral soon gained distinction and inspired imitation, both at home and abroad. Indeed, owing to its rib-vaults, pointed transverse arches in the nave, and supposed proto-flying buttresses in the nave gallery, Durham is sometimes viewed as a precursor of Gothic architecture which developed in France in the mid 12th century. What is certain is that it is undoubtedly one of the greatest of all Romanesque cathedrals - a superb and enduring reminder of the skills and aspirations of a bygone age.

ESCOMB CHURCH

T he Church of St John the Evangelist lies in the heart of the village of Escomb, near Bishop Auckland, and is a building of more than local significance for it is one of the oldest and most complete Anglo-Saxon churches in England: a celebrated survival from the early days of Christianity in the North East.

The date of its construction is uncertain. It has been suggested that St John's dates from the mid 7th century and owes its origin to the zealous preaching work of Irish missionaries, who were the dominant Christian influence in Northumbria from 635 when Aidan founded a monastery on Lindisfarne until the synod of Whitby in 664. Its circular churchyard is said, among other things, to support this view. But others favour a later date. For instance, in a survey dating from the 14th century there is a reference to land at Escomb called 'St Wolfrid's Acre', and it has thus been suggested that Escomb Church was founded by St Wilfrid (634-709), though some favour a date well in the 8th century on the grounds that Bede (c.673-735) does not mention St John's in his writings. But Bede only mentions churches connected with events that he is discussing, and it seems probable, owing to some similarities with churches founded in the days of Bede, that St. John's was built in the late 7th or early 8th century.

In the latter half of the 19th century St John's was reduced to the status of a chapel following the construction of a new parish church in the village in 1863, and as such suffered from neglect. But in 1875 its historical value was fully realised and restoration work commenced, with the result that it was reopened for worship on 4 October 1880 by Bishop Lightfoot. In 1970 it once again became the parish church: the Victorian church, whose fabric was deteriorating, was demolished the following year.

Description

Escomb Church is approached from the south, and is a well built but spartan structure, aptly described by the late Sir Frank Stenton as 'a work of austere dignity'.

It has a tall and narrow nave, (like other early Northumbrian churches such as St Peter's, Monkwearmouth), and a chancel which is narrower than the nave. The masonry is largely composed of substantial stones believed to have been brought to Escomb from the ruins of the nearby Roman fort at Binchester, and have diamond-broaching typical of Roman work. The quoins are side-alternate, and particularly massive.

Two of the windows in the south wall of the nave are original. They both have a large rectangular stone forming the sill, two narrower rectangular slabs forming the jambs (which slope inward from bottom to top), while the lintel is a large rectangular stone which has been cut into in order to form the round head of the window. Between these windows is an Anglo-Saxon sundial and according to H.M and J. Taylor, it is 'almost certainly the oldest now in its original setting in the walls of a building.' It is ornamented by a snake-like creature which partly surrounds it, and above which is a sculpted beast's head. Nicholas Beddow has recently commented that the 'sundial suggests a faith which was not afraid of pagan symbols.'

Excavations in 1968 revealed that a porticus had been attached to the north side of the chancel. Fragments of window glass were found, and some of these are identical to fragments found at Monkwearmouth and Jarrow, the famed 'monastery in two places' established by Benedict Biscop in the late 7th century.

Midway up, towards the east end of north wall of the nave, is an upside down stone from Binchester which bears the inscription 'LEG VI,' i.e., the Sixth Legion. This wall has two small original windows similar to those in the south wall of the nave, but they are square-headed. The wall also has a square-headed doorway which is evidently original and interesting for the upper stone of each jamb is mortised into the lintel in a manner suggesting woodwork.

The excavations of 1968 uncovered the foundations of what had been a two-storey annexe adjoining the west end of the nave. Like the porticus, it was not bonded into the fabric of the church. Its roof-line can still be seen when viewing the exterior of the west wall. Here one can also see an original window high up in the gable. It is small and round-headed.

The church is entered through a porch against the south wall of the nave. It is a post-Conquest addition (according to Pevsner it was probably built in the 14th century), and is evidently comprised of stones which had belonged to the west annexe.

The nave measures 43½ft by 14½ft and is about 23ft high. At its west end is a patch of cobble flooring which may very well date from the church's construction. Formerly, the original deeply splayed windows had wooden shutters, and the jambs still have the vertical grooves which held them. The nave was whitewashed in the 1960s.

The chancel, which is 10ft square, received the same treatment. It is generally accepted that the impressive chancel arch was brought to Escomb from Binchester. However, the arrangement of the stones of its jambs, alternately upright and flat, is typically Anglo-Saxon and is known as 'Escomb fashion', a name coined by a pioneering figure in the study of Anglo-Saxon architecture, Baldwin Brown.

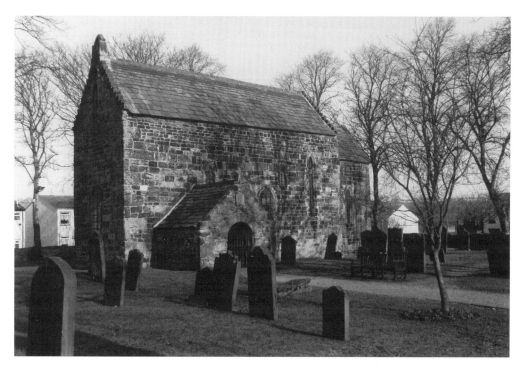

36. Escomb Church from the south

FINCHALE PRIORY

T he picturesque ruins of Finchale Priory (pronounced 'Finkle') nestle in a loop of the River Wear and are overlooked by high ground. This is particularly true to the north where cliffs rise precipitously and are crowned by ancient woodland, which is likewise a feature of the east bank, again opposite the ruins.

The story of Finchale begins with St Godric, a colourful figure born near the Wash in 1065, who became a much-travelled merchant with trading links in countries as far apart as Denmark and the Holy Land. Moreover, it is sometimes said that he was the 'Guderic, a pirate from the kingdom of England', who gave the King of Jerusalem a lift from Arsuf to Jaffa in 1102. What is certain is that he had religious inclinations, for he undertook pilgrimages to Rome and visited shrines such as that of St James at Compostela, Spain.

In about 1104 he began living a solitary life of religious devotion near Carlisle. He then moved east to Wolsingham and lived with an elderly hermit and, whilst doing so, is said to have been told in a vision that St Cuthbert would provide him with a place for a hermitage of his own at Finchale. But upon his companion's death in 1106, he revisited Rome before spending time at Whitby. He then journeyed north to Durham and in about 1112 began residing at Finchale with the blessing of Bishop Flambard who had granted him the site. Godric built a small hut and an adjoining chapel and, following a flood in 1149, constructed a more substantial place of worship which was dedicated to John the Baptist by Bishop Geoffrey Rufus.

At some point, likely not long after settling at Finchale, Godric was joined by his sister, Burcwen, who wished to live a life of prayer and asceticism. She did so within earshot of his cell for many years, until she was moved by the almoner of Durham Priory to the hospital of St Giles in Durham where she spent the rest of her life.

Burcwen's removal appears to have occurred after Godric had accepted the supervision of Durham Priory. He did so at the suggestion of others, (likely Durham monks), who told him that obedience was an essential feature of the religious life. He submitted himself to the authority of a friend, Prior Roger of Durham, and it appears that this was an informal arrangement for after Roger's death in 1149 Godric chose the Priors of Durham as his superiors.

From members of the Durham community Godric received instruction. Furthermore monks were sent to Finchale on a regular basis to say Mass. Moreover, as old age rendered Godric increasingly infirm, one monk or more was sent to live with him and visitors could only speak to him with the permission of the resident monk. In short, according to his principal biographer and contemporary, Reginald of Durham, Godric was a monk of Durham and thus subject to its authority. Evidently he had made no profession, and so we should no doubt view him as an 'associate monk' rather than as a full member of the house.

Godric died at Finchale on 21 May 1170 at the age of 105, and following his death his hermitage was used as such by Durham monks. Then, in 1196, it was decided to found a dependent house of Durham at Finchale. The man responsible for founding Finchale Priory, Henry du Puiset, was of baronial status and had initially founded a house for Augustinian canons elsewhere in County Durham but had encountered opposition from the powerful monks of Durham Priory who were only agreeable to the establishment of

37. Aerial view of Finchale Priory from the south

another Benedictine house. He thus terminated his fledgling foundation and granted its possessions to Finchale, which was then given to him on condition that he establish a Benedictine community here. Initially, only temporary structures were erected, but in about 1237 work commenced on a grander scale and continued until late in the century.

By the time Finchale Priory was founded, Godric's tomb had become a place of pilgrimage, for he had enjoyed a reputation for sanctity in his lifetime and this had grown following his death. Hence, although he never received papal canonization, he was viewed as a saint by many in the region and ill layfolk visited Finchale in the hope of receiving miraculous cures at his tomb - there does not appear to have been a shrine. The first person to be miraculously cured was an epileptic child on 23 June 1172. Reginald of Durham records over 200 such miracles at Finchale, and according to R. Finucane, around 10 per cent of the known pilgrims (most of whom lived within thirty miles of the priory), had visited a physician before resting their hopes on a miraculous cure. Further-more, many had visited several shrines, that of St Thomas Becket at Canterbury for instance, before making their way here in the hope that they would at last obtain relief. Moreover, 70 per cent of those said to have been cured were female. Women were excluded from St Cuthbert's shrine at Durham, and it thus seems likely that the majority of those who sought a cure at Finchale were female.

The number of monks at Finchale was always small, peaking at fifteen in 1278. During the 14th century it was decided to make Finchale a retreat for monks from the mother house. Just when Finchale became a 'holiday place' is unknown, but a reference of 1346 shows that the practice was well established. It is also interesting to note that in the mid 14th century the Prior of Durham had to reprimand the monks for keeping a pack of hounds, something which indicates that more adventurous pursuits were undertaken here than was intended. In 1408 it was stipulated that monks from Durham would travel to Finchale in groups of four and spend three weeks in the company of the resident community, a prior and four monks, before being replaced by another party. On alternate days the visiting monks either had to keep the usual round of services or had leave to walk 'religiously and honestly' in the fields except for having to attend Mass and Vespers: a routine they conducted in pairs.

Finchale remained a retreat for monks from Durham until the Dissolution of the Monasteries when it was surrendered into royal hands in 1538, later than most other houses with annual incomes under £200.

Description

The most scenic approach to Finchale Priory is from the opposite bank of the river. A pathway through Cocken Wood, to the north and east of the ruins, leads down from the roadside to the Wear and offers glimpses of the site through the trees, before heading along the river bank to a wooden footbridge which gives access to the site. Unfortunately though, increasing car theft has rendered it best to drive directly to Finchale instead.

The ruins contain much of interest. The church has a typical east-west axis and is 195ft long and 99ft across the transepts. The chancel had three lancet windows in its east end near to which was a wooden screen. The narrow space to the east of this served as a vestry, while to the west of the screen was the presbytery with the high altar reach by four steps. At the west end of the chancel was the choir.

Initially the chancel had aisles with cylindrical arcade piers, (two on the north side have well executed stiff-leaf capitals with fir cones), but in the mid 1360s the aisles were demolished - presumably to save the cost of repairs - and the arcades filled in and

38. The prior's house (left) and the east end of the church, (right). In the foreground are the remains of the bakehouse and the brewhouse

provided with three-light windows with an old-fashioned motif - reticulated tracery.

An interesting feature of the chancel is that it contains the outline in the grass of St Godric's Chapel of St John which was superseded by the church. A stone cross marks the site where Godric was buried.

The crossing was the only part of the church with a vault, and was surmounted by a low tower with a spire. The tower was supported by four cylindrical piers. Of these the north-west pier is the largest - it is over 7ft in diameter - and contains a newel stair which ascended to the tower.

On the east side of the north transept is a blocked opening which gave access to the Chapel of St Godric. (The chapel was contemporary with the church, and like the aisles referred to above, was demolished in the mid 1360s). On the west side of the transept are two very tall lancets characteristic of the northern Early English style.

The south transept served as St Mary's Chapel and in the east wall, above where the altar dedicated to the Virgin stood, a large window was inserted in about 1300. Against the south wall was a staircase leading to the monks' dormitory in the east claustral range.

And what of the nave? It is shorter than the chancel, but likewise had aisles. Originally it was intended that the arcades would spring from the west piers of the crossing tower but, no doubt to provide additional abutment for the tower, solid walls were built west from the piers with the result that the arcades sprang from responds about 8ft further west than first planned. The north aisle was demolished in the mid 1360s and the arcade provided with three-light windows with reticulated tracery. However, the south aisle was transformed into the north walk of the cloister, replacing the original north walk which was pulled down.

The cloister was originally 75ft square and had open arcades towards the garth. In the 14th century, though, it was enlarged and provided with traceried windows. The claustral buildings comprise an east and south range.

The principal chamber at ground-floor level in the east range is the chapter house, which adjoins the south transept. It still has its entrance arch with flanking windows, and around the walls one can see the stone seats upon which the monks sat. To the south are the remains of three rooms. The first was probably a parlour and the second a larder, while it has been suggested that the third and largest chamber was the warming room. The dormitory occupied the upper floor of the range.

The vaulting of the undercroft of the south range has heavy ribs supported against the walls by keeled responds, and by octagonal piers without capitals along the centre of the undercroft. A doorway with an arch of three orders and a nook shaft in each jamb gives access from near the west end of the south walk of the cloister to the floor above which contained the refectory, which is a rebuilding dating from c.1320. It has four widely spaced lancets overlooking the cloister and five windows in its south wall. The western half of the refectory was soon divided into two storeys of chambers and then, perhaps in the 15th century, the eastern half was provided with an upper storey. It seems probable that by this date the monks had ceased dining here and ate in the prior's hall to the east of the east range instead.

Against the outer face of the west wall of the cloister, and close to the west end of the church, are the remains of a two-storey structure attributed to the 14th century which is known as the 'Guest house' because it has been conjectured that it functioned as such. Recently, however, P.R. Wilson has highlighted that although some of the fabric dates from the 14th century this is not necessarily true of it in its entirety for the building has undoubtedly experienced substantial alterations. It evidently once extended further along the west side of the cloister and was likely part of a west claustral range. It has

some architectural preten-
sions and Wilson has thus
commented that it may
have been altered to serve
as a new prior's house in
the days when Finchale was
a 'holiday home' for Dur-
ham monks who, as noted
above, are believed to have
eaten (and spent much of
their time) in the prior's
house mentioned earlier.

39. Finchale Priory in the 19th century

And what of buildings to
the east of the claustral
ranges? One such is the
reredorter, which adjoins
the south-east end of the
east range. This is adjoined
to the north by the kitchen,
which is also against the
east range. The remains of
an oven are clearly visible.
The kitchen dates from the
15th century and was no doubt constructed here because by this date the monks had
taken to dining in the adjacent prior's hall rather than in the refectory. Where the earlier
kitchen was is unknown. The usual site would have been adjoining the west end of the
refectory but excavation there has proved unfruitful.

The prior's hall adjoined the east end of the kitchen and was in a long range running
east. For at least much of the priory's history the range formed the house of the prior and
was of two storeys, with the vaulted lower storey principally being used as cellarage:
some of the vaulting survives at the east end. The prior's hall occupied virtually the entire
western half of the upper floor. To the east was a solar with a fine two-light east window
with geometrical tracery. Branching off north at the east end of the solar was a study
with an oriel window on its north side, while branching off to the south of the solar was
the prior's chapel with a straight-headed east window of three lights.

To the east of this range are the foundations of the brewhouse and the bakehouse,
while to the north of the prior's study (and to the east of the church) are the remains of
the temporary buildings constructed between 1196 and 1237. The survival of such
temporary structures is a rare feature: later building work usually led to their obliteration.
Little can be made out but it appears there was a central hall, with a solar and garderobe
to the south and a solar to the north.

Finchale Priory is cared for by English Heritage and thus contrasts with its condition in
the last century when it was visited by W.S. Gibson, who wrote: 'To the architect, no less
than to the antiquary, these ruins are full of interest....Unpeopled and desecrated for
three centuries, time has spead over the chief portions of these walls, a mantle of
venerable and luxuriant ivy, whose roots entwine about the foundations...when all
besides is crumbling to ruins.'

GIBSIDE CHAPEL

Gibside Chapel is an architectural gem. It lies in pleasant parkland in the valley of the River Derwent some seven miles south-west of Gateshead and was part of one of County Durham's finest estates - Gibside - which enjoyed its greatest days in the 18th and 19th centuries. Work on the chapel began in 1760 when Gibside was owned by George Bowes, a colourful individual whose father, Sir William Bowes of Streatlam near Barnard Castle, had acquired the estate through marriage in 1691.

George Bowes became head of the family in 1722 at the age of twenty-one upon the death of a brother, and was a man of wide interests. As his Gibside estate overlay important coal seams - first worked in the 17th century - in 1726 he became a member of an important partnership of local coalowners, The Grand Allies, aimed at maximizing the profits which could be accrued from the coal trade. Moreover he represented Durham in parliament as a Whig from 1727 until his death in 1760, and though only one speech is recorded as having been made by him in the Commons, was an active lobbyist on behalf of the coal trade. Rural pursuits and sport also engaged his attention: he introduced fox hunting into County Durham in 1738 and, like his father, was a devotee of horse-breeding and racing. Furthermore, he was interested in both architecture and music.

Although he styled himself George Bowes of Streatlam, it was the Gibside estate which received most of his attention. Indeed, Gibside was his principal residence (he only visited Streatlam occasionally) and made changes both to the Jacobean house and the grounds. For a start, shortly after inheriting the property, he removed a settlement which had grown up to the east of the hall. He also undertook measures to enhance the estate by, for example, purchasing adjoining land, planting trees, and laying out straight walks and rides near the house, including a half-mile avenue over 60ft wide known as the Grand Walk (made in 1746-9) along which he exercised his horses.

Other changes included the construction of a 'Gothick' banqueting house in the first half of the 1740s, and Palladian fronted stables in 1747-51, both designed by Daniel Garrett. Evidently Garrett also designed what is known as the Column of British Liberty, situated near the north-east end of the Hollow Walk, a short continuation of the Grand Walk. It was begun in 1750 and was completed in 1759 by James Paine, who took over the work in 1753 upon Garrett's death. It rises to a total height of just over 146ft and like Nelson's Column in London, which it slightly exceeds in height, is surmounted by a statue.

Moreover, in 1759 Paine was commissioned to construct a chapel at the opposite end of the avenue. The idea of building a chapel was not a new one. Bowes had entertained thoughts of doing so in the 1730s - a plan was in fact drawn up in 1737 - but nothing came of the project for Bowes concentrated on other things. Then, on 7 February 1750, he again expressed a desire for a chapel to be built. He did so within a year of the birth of a daughter, Mary Eleanor, when drawing up his will. He declared that his daughter's trustees should use the annual profit from his collieries to 'lay out the Sum of Two Thousand Pounds in Building a Chappel at the West End of the Great Walk [i.e., Grand Walk], at Gibside which Sum shall be so laid out within the space of six years after my death.' Furthermore, after stipulating the salary of the minister, he continued: 'And my further will is that a good Vault be made in the said Chappell where I desire I may be buried.'

40. Gibside Chapel

Winning stones for the chapel from nearby quarries commenced in November 1759, and in July of the following year work on the foundations began. By this date George Bowes was nearing his end. He had been ill for some time, and was to die on 17 September 1760, leaving eleven-year-old Mary Eleanor as his heir. Responsibility for continuing work on the chapel fell to the trustees, though Bowes' widow took an interest in the project.

Work on the chapel continued for some years and during this period Mary Eleanor met a Scottish peer, John Lyon, the ninth Earl of Strathmore, whose mother was the daughter of a Durham gentleman, James Nicholson of West Rainton. Strathmore was a handsome individual (he was known as 'The Beautiful') and was intelligent and learned, something which appealed to Mary Eleanor who largely thanks to the encouragement of her late father, was an accomplished young lady, particularly knowledgeable about botany and languages.

A marriage between the couple was decided upon by June 1766. Bowes had stipulated in his will that whoever married Mary Eleanor would not gain possession of the estates and annual income of £20,000 unless he assumed the name of Bowes and thus Strathmore duly complied. The marriage took place on Mary's eighteenth birthday, 24 February 1767, at St George's Square, Hanover. By this date the chapel at Gibside had been erected. Decorative work internally, however, still needed to be finished. But in 1769 work on the

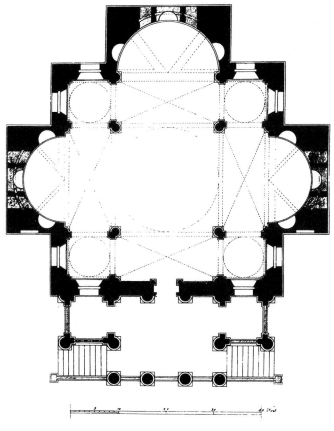

Plan of the Chaple, underneath is a Mausoleum, built in the Plantations at Gibside.

41. Paine's plan of the chapel

chapel ceased before the project had been completed, with more than double what George Bowes had allocated in his will having been spent on the undertaking.

The Earl and Countess of Strathmore had five children. However, owing to the different temperaments of the couple, their marriage did not prove a happy one. Indeed, when the earl died at sea of consumption on 7 March 1776 the countess received news of his death with indifference.

She soon met and married an unscrupulous character called Andrew Robinson Stoney, an army lieutenant on half pay, who likewise assumed the name Bowes. The marriage took place on 17 January 1777. Stoney Bowes, as he was called, was a cruel gold digger who proceeded to entertain lavishly at Gibside, squandered money in other ways, and felled many trees on the estate in order to obtain money to pay his debts. Moreover, he treated Mary Eleanor in a heartless and shameless manner, (he had caused the death of a previous wife by mistreatment), with the result that she escaped from him in 1785 and obtained a divorce in 1789.

The following year her eldest son, the tenth Earl of Strathmore came of age, and in subsequent years the condition of the neglected and despoiled Gibside estate improved. Furthermore, he made alterations to Gibside Hall and in January 1811 resumed work on the chapel, which was consecrated in 1812, whereupon George Bowes' body was transferred from nearby Whickham and interred in the mausoleum beneath the chapel.

The tenth Earl of Strathmore died in 1820, within hours of marrying a woman of humble birth with whom he had lived for many years, mostly at Streatlam, and by whom he had had an illegitimate son, John Bowes. In due course, the widowed countess remarried and used Gibside as a residence in preference to Streatlam Castle. She died in 1860, and her son followed her to the grave in 1885, whereupon his property passed to the thirteenth Earl of Strathmore.

In 1965 the sixteenth earl gave Gibside Chapel and part of the estate to the National Trust, and in 1993 the Trust bought the remainder of the estate from the eighteenth earl.

Description

Gibside Chapel is situated at the south-west end of the Grand Walk. It is exquisite, and architecturally has always been the most impressive feature of the estate. It is Classical in style and owes much to Palladio.

In plan, the chapel is a Greek cross with one arm - the northernmost - flattened to form the entrance. The exterior is essentially plain with the exception of the entrance facade which has an impressive double portico reached by balustraded steps. There are six giant engaged columns with Ionic capitals, while four other giant Ionic columns, which have balustrading along their inner face, stand forward from the body of the chapel and carry a pediment in front of a plain parapet crowned by four urns. Higher up, above the centre of the chapel, is a tall drum ornamented with festoons and crowned by a shallow dome.

Internally, three apses radiate from a central area and have groin-vaulted ceilings, while in the angles between the apses and the domed centre of the chapel are low domed spaces. The interior is spacious, well-lit, and elegant. The walls are painted in pale colours, while the architectural features such as the enriched entablature and the capitals of the composite columns which support the central dome are in white. The interior is, however, not exactly as Paine had planned. For example, he intended the vaults and dome to be coffered and that niches in the apses (there are three in each apse) would contain statues, something which would have rendered the chapel more vibrant and imposing.

All the furnishings date from the early 19th century, with the main ones being of cherry-wood. In the centre of the chapel, and surrounded by rails, is the communion table. To the left of this is an oval three-decker pulpit with an umbrella-shaped sounding-board supported by an Ionic column, while in the apses and corners of the chapel are box pews. The former, with curved seats, were used by servants and visitors whilst the latter were for the family, agent and chaplain.

After visiting the chapel one can enjoy extensive walks in the grounds, and in so doing see several points of interest, including the Column of Liberty and the ruins of Gibside Hall.

HOLY TRINITY CHURCH, SUNDERLAND

An Act of Parliament which came into effect on I May 1719 created the 'Parish of Sunderland near the Sea.' It states, 'the...Town of Sunderland being a large and populous Town, containing six thousand souls, and upwards...is become a place of great trade and commerce, and the families daily increasing...they, the said inhabitants...at their very great expense, and by the voluntary contributions of several neighbouring gentlemen, and by money collected by a Brief, have erected and built a beautiful Church...'

Holy Trinity Church was subsequently consecrated on 5 September by the Bishop of London, for Durham's own bishop, elderly Nathaniel Crewe, was too frail to officiate. Holy Trinity was to serve a parish 178 acres in extent, on the south side of the mouth of the River Wear, carved out of the huge ancient parish of Bishopwearmouth which consisted of 'divers Townships, Villages and hamlets.' Hitherto, Sunderland's Anglicans had had to make their way up a long and fairly steep incline to the parish church of Bishopwearmouth, St Michael's, situated about half a mile from the western outskirts of Sunderland. This, and the fact that St Michael's was too small to accommodate more than a fraction of the locality's Anglicans, contributed to the desire of Sunderland folk to have their own church and parish. But there was another reason. At this date parishes were units of local government - through their select vestries - and members of Sunderland's vibrant community wished to be in charge of their own affairs.

Who designed the church? Daniel Newcome, the first rector, is credited by one source as having been the 'principal architect', but it is generally accepted that this honour should be accorded to William Etty of York. At the very least, he was responsible for fitting out and decorating the interior. Etty was an able man, a master carpenter, a skilled wood carver, and an architect familiar with work by the foremost early 18th century English architects, Sir John Vanbrugh and Nicholas Hawksmoor. He had served as Vanbrugh's clerk of works at Castle Howard in Yorkshire and was soon, if he had already not done so, to begin holding the same position at another of Vanbrugh's masterpieces, Seaton Delaval in Northumberland.

Holy Trinity was built in a rather secluded setting on the edge of the Town Moor a short distance to the south of the east end of Sunderland's principal thoroughfare, High Street. To the east and south of the church was the Town Moor, whilst just to the west were burgage garths of properties running along the south side of the High Street, some of which had begun to be built on to meet the needs of Sunderland's expanding population.

At the time of Holy Trinity's construction, and for many years to come, the parish of Sunderland's population was a diverse one consisting of people ranging from the destitute to the affluent. Among the latter were coal fitters, individuals involved in the trade which dominated the commercial life of Sunderland and for more than a century before Holy Trinity's construction, had been chiefly responsible for its rise from obscurity to a place of some consequence. In terms of religion, the population was likewise not uniform. In addition to the Anglicans who worshipped in Holy Trinity (and in the daughter church of St John's from 1767), were Dissenters such as Catholics, Quakers, and Presbyterians, who worshipped in a number of establishments, which at least at the time of Holy Trinity's construction were nondescript. Moreover from the mid 18th century onward Sunderland had a vibrant Methodist community.

As the parish became increasingly populous and industrial, many wealthy folk moved west to more pleasant surroundings in Bishopwearmouth parish. The once fine houses near Holy Trinity thus either became, or were soon to become, tenements. An appalling slum was in the making.

In his *Spas of England: the North*, (published in 1841), Dr Augustus Granville appropriately described part of the parish as 'the very sink of gloom and filth - an apt nest or rendezvous for typhus and cholera.' Typhus had recently carried off a number of inhabitants, as had cholera. The first cholera victims died in late 1831 when Wearside was the first place struck by Britain's first outbreak of Asiatic Cholera, and the area most severely hit on Wearside was the parish of Sunderland. 156 of the 202 locals who perished lived in the parish. The Rector of Sunderland at the time was the Reverend Robert Gray, and he behaved admirably. William Brockie relates that he 'took a most active part in visiting the sick during the period of the pestilence, for a period of four months,' declaring: 'I will rely upon this trust, that the man who fears God has nothing else to fear.'

Gray subsequently died of typhus in February 1838 after catching the disease while ministering to the needs of victims of a typhus epidemic which had struck Sunderland. *The Sunderland Herald* of February 24th sadly noted that 'no town in the Empire ever sustained a heavier loss by the death of an individual than Sunderland has now to deplore on the removal of so holy and zealous a pastor.' He was buried in the churchground of Holy Trinity and his funeral was a splendid affair. Between twenty and thirty thousand people are said to have assembled for the occasion. Brockie comments that 'An idea may be formed of the magnitude of the long line of mourners, when it is stated that when the leading part of the procession had reached the Church, a distance of more than half a mile, the rear of it had scarcely begun to move from the residence of the deceased in Sunniside.' (Gray had preferred to live in that part of Sunderland rather than Holy Trinity's rectory).

Despite efforts to improve conditions in the 'east end', as the area of Sunderland in which Holy Trinity is situated became known, it remained a slum into the 20th century when things greatly improved largely owing to the removal of many of the inhabitants to peripheral council estates.

The clearances, combined with declining religious attendance in general, inevitably affected Holy Trinity and in the 1970s it ceased to function as a parish church when it began to be served by the clergy of a Victorian church, St Ignatius. In 1988 the decision was taken to close Holy Trinity and it was handed over to the Redundant Churches Fund which has carried out much needed restoration work and the occasional service is still held, particularly on Trinity Sundays.

Description

The church is built of small handmade bricks while sandstone is used for dressings. Brick was not widely used in County Durham at the time. Indeed, along with Stockton Parish Church (1710-12), Holy Trinity was the largest building in the county then built of brick.

The exterior is not particularly striking. It is nonetheless fairly elegant and possesses a quiet charm. The dominant feature is the tower. This is of four stages, with the base stage consisting of the principal west porch. The doorway of this porch is flanked by Tuscan pilasters, while the second stage of the tower has a large round-headed window flanked by niches. The third stage has, on each side, a clock face, while the fourth stage contains louvred belfry windows. The tower is surmounted by stone pinnacles at each corner. Prior to 1738 there was also a cupola but this was dismantled after becoming ruinous.

The north and south sides of the church are dominated by seven substantial round-headed windows whose glass is plain, while from the centre of the east side of the church protrudes an apsidal chancel added by Newcome in 1735.

The church is entered by the northernmost of the three west doorways. In the north-west porch is a brass plaque commemorating Jack Crawford who died on 9 November 1831 shortly after contracting cholera. Of humble birth, Crawford made his name at the Battle of Camperdown in 1797 while serving on HMS *Venerable.* In the fierce action Admiral Duncan's colours were shot away by Dutch cannon, whereupon Crawford seized the flag, scaled the main mast, and nailed the flag back in place, an action which made him a national hero.

From the porch a fine stair leads up to the west gallery, and also gives access to steps ascending to the rooms in the tower such as the bell ringers' chamber.

At ground floor level, after emerging from the porch, one arrives in the vestibule which runs right across the full width of the church. The attractive font is located here and above this, in the low ceiling, is a small dome painted with cherubs and around the circumference of which is the following text: 'Suffer the little children to come unto me for of such is the kingdom of heaven.'

Immediately to the west of the font is the substantial central porch. It is dominated by a very impressive memorial of the Reverend Robert Gray by David Dunbar of Carlisle. The more than life-sized statue depicts Gray in a long gown, cravat and bands, with a sheaf of papers in hand, and is flanked by reliefs of Faith and Charity, both young women with children. The parochial stocks were housed in the porch for many years, as was a rudimentary fire engine, for in accordance with an Act of Parliament of 1704 the parish had to have its own firefighting equipment.

To the south of the central porch, and entered from the vestibule, is the vestry. Prior to 1835 when Sunderland was created a municipal borough, local government was conducted here under the chairmanship of the rector by the 'gentlemen of the vestry,' twenty-four individuals of some substance who were elected every three years by fellow ratepayers. Among other things, they raised rates, saw to the maintenance of the church, and appointed paro chial officers such as a scavenger who cleaned the streets. The large oak leaved table around which they sat is still in situ.

42. The west front of Holy Trinity Church

43. Interior view of Holy Trinity, looking east

At the south end of the vestibule are alternative stairs to the west gallery. These also lead up to what was the library located above the vestry. A large book-case with writing and reading desks can be seen on the north wall, a reminder of the days when this room housed what was probably Sunderland's first public library.

Initially, the west gallery had short extensions along the north and south walls, but in 1842 these were replaced by large galleries which added 320 free seats to the church's previous total of 1,193 seats, 242 of which were free. The side galleries are, however, no longer extant. A small gallery for the choir located above the west gallery is likewise no longer in existence.

The front of the west gallery is adorned by three coats of arms, those of George I, Bishop Crewe of Durham and Dr John Robinson of London, which can only be seen well from the nave. Nonetheless, the gallery provides excellent views of the body of the church. Spaciousness, light and elegance, are hallmarks of the interior. Two parallel rows of tall Corinthian columns, which support the plain ceiling, lead the eye towards the imposing chancel arch, the crowning glory of the interior. It has two pairs of fluted Corinthian columns with carved plinths, and elaborate plasterwork depicting cherubs, an open Bible, and two Durham episcopal mitres.

The slightly elliptical chancel is entered via three Frosterley marble steps, and as noted earlier, dates from 1735. Prior to its construction a shallow bay at the east end of the church contained the altar. The altar is, of course, now situated in the chancel which is lit by a substantial Venetian window at its east end.

Holy Trinity is an important example of an early Georgian church and as Geoffrey Milburn has commented, when built 'must have seemed very much a symbol of the age of reason and modernity' in comparison to the old neighbouring churches of St Michael's, Bishopwearmouth, and St Peter's, Monkwearmouth, and 'a monument to the civic pride and commercial progress of the busy, populous new parish.'

HYLTON CASTLE

ylton Castle is situated a short distance to the north of the River Wear on the north-west outskirts of Sunderland, and has a grim and rather forbidding aspect. For centuries it was the seat of the Hylton family, which legend states was of Saxon origin. However, the first member of the line of whom we have authentic record was 'Romanus de Helton' who made an agreement with the Prior and Chapter of Durham in 1157, whereby he could have a chaplain at Hylton provided that he (and his successors), did not neglect the parish church of St Peter, Monkwearmouth, which among other things had to be attended for major Church festivals such as Christmas.

In 1166 it was recorded that Hylton held 3 knights' fees of 'old enfeoffment' from his lord, the bishop, a fairly substantial feudal holding which made him one of Hugh du Puiset's principal vassals. The fact that the fees were of 'old enfeoffment' means that they were granted between the Conquest and 1135 and this most likely occurred during the episcopate of Ranulf Flambard (1099-1128), when the majority of such fees in County Durham were granted. Initially, the Hyltons' lands were confined to the Sunderland area, but in time estates were acquired further afield such as in Northumberland, Yorkshire and Suffolk.

Many members of the line inevitably participated in military ventures. During the Barons' War of the mid 1260s, for instance, the then head of the family, Sir Robert de Hylton, sided with the rebels. His name appears on a list of Durham knights who fought at the Battle of Lewes in 1264 (when an outnumbered rebel army routed that of King Henry III), and in 1266 - by which time the Royalist cause was in the ascendant - he helped his kinsman, John de Vescy, capture Alnwick Castle. Hence a document of the time states that 'Robert de Hylton is in the Castle of Alnwick in arms against the king.' In 1271 he received a full pardon.

From the late 12th century the Hyltons ranked as barons of the bishopric, i.e., they were senior tenants of the Bishop of Durham and attended his assemblies and councils and had a say in the administration of the bishopric. Moreover, it is sometimes maintained that the Hyltons were peers of the realm from the late 13th century until the mid 15th century when the title is said to have been forfeited. But the evidence does not support this. It is certainly true that in 1295, during the reign of Edward I, the then head of the family, Sir Robert, (probably the veteran of the Barons' War), was summoned to parliament by name, the first of the line to receive such a summons. Some argue that persons summoned to parliament by individual writ automatically became peers of the realm, but H.A. Doubleday of *The Complete Peerage* has declared: 'From the time of Edward I, a great number of men were summoned to parliament by individual writ. Modern law holds that peerages were so created. But the idea that Edward I...should create seventy or eighty [barons] in one day is laughable.' Furthermore, as May McKisack has commented, 'a carefully delimited hereditary peerage' with an 'exclusive right' of summons to parliament was not yet in existence. She is speaking of the 14th century, but the quotation is of course applicable to the late 13th century. The number of people who received such summonses undoubtedly fluctuated greatly: Edward II, for instance, summoned ninety 'barons' in 1321 and only 52 in the following year and while members of certain families were regularly summoned, and thus can be viewed as of genuinely baronial status, only three Hyltons received such summonses and they were not regu-larly called upon to attend parliament.

The last member of the Hylton family to receive a personal writ of summons to parliament was called William. He was born in Alnwick Castle in 1355 and was respon-sible for building Hylton Castle in the late 14th and early 15th centuries. He had a rather adventurous life. In 1383, for example, during the Hundred Years War, he volunteered to serve on an ill-fated expedition to Flanders. Moreover, according to the chronicler, Jean Froissart, (who was well acquainted with the engagement), in 1388 Hylton was captured by the Scots at Otterburn, a battle which ended disastrously for the English. Furthermore, it seems likely that he also participated in the overthrow of Richard II in 1399. In that year Richard's exiled kinsman, Henry of Lancaster, returned to England and was joined by 'all the people of the north country.' The unpopular king was soon made captive and writs were then issued in his name summoning people to attend parliament on the last day of September. One of the writs was sent to Hylton - the first and last occasion he received such a writ - and it thus seems probable that he had thrown in his lot with Henry, whose claim to the throne was accepted by parliament that autumn.

In 1536 another head of the line, Sir Thomas, participated in an unsuccessful rebellion known as the Pilgrimage of Grace. Indeed, he was one of four delegates sent by the rebels to state their grievances to Henry VIII's lieutenant, the Duke of Norfolk, at Doncaster. Evidently, like some other principal figures in the revolt, he was not enthusiastic about the rising, and in 1539 Henry granted him the lands of the recently dissolved Tynemouth Priory. Furthermore, he was later appointed Captain of Tynemouth Castle during the reign of Edward VI (1547-53).

In 1569 another unsuccessful Catholic rising occurred. On this occasion the head of the Hylton family, Sir Robert, rallied to the side of the Crown, one of the few Durham notables to do so. It is thus ironic that in 1593 his wife was reported to the government by one of its spies for celebrating Mass, presumably at Hylton Castle.

During the Civil War the Hyltons fought for the king. By this date the family's estates had been bequeathed to the City of London for 99 years by Henry Hylton (who had died in 1641), who wished them to be administered for charitable purposes. Under the terms of his will a modest annuity was to be paid to his successor, a brother. But fortunately for the family, control of the estates was restored to a nephew of Henry's in the 1660s following extensive litigation.

In 1746, (by which time Hylton Castle had recently been transformed, principally by the addition of three-storey Classical wings), the last of the Hyltons died and the estates passed to a brother-in-law, Sir Richard Musgrave, who soon sold Hylton Castle to Mrs Bowes of Streatlam and Gibside. In the mid 19th century the castle was purchased by a local businessman, William Briggs, who demolished the wings and, among other things, inserted new floor arrangements in the historic core of the castle as well as the Gothic windows seen today.

By the 1950s the castle's interior was in such a dilapidated state that the Ministry of Works decided to replace Briggs' internal partitions and turn it into a shell in which all the surviving medieval features could be seen by visitors.

Description

Hylton Castle is 59ft high with turrets projecting a further 10ft, measures around 75ft from north to south by about 45ft, has walls up to 9ft thick, and belongs to a group of castles known as tower-houses. Castles of this type were first built in England in the early

44. Hylton Castle from the north-west by Turner

14th century and were especially popular in the North. They are generally unspectacular, (they were seldom the residences of magnates), and have been likened to manor houses stuck on end. Tattershall in Lincolnshire is a well known example of a tower-house castle, and though not as substantial, in its heyday Hylton was one of the finest tower-house castles in England. It was built in the form of a greatly enlarged gatehouse, and as Beric Morley has stated, its 'internal arrangements made it remarkably self-contained...it would have been possible for a family of some distinction to live quite satisfactorily [within it] save only for such ancillary buildings as the stabling, a brewhouse, barns etc.'

The west front is the most imposing. The entrance is located here and was originally defended by a portcullis. There are four square turrets, two flanking the arched entrance, and one at each corner. The turrets are crowned by octagonal battlemented and machicolated parapets which were once adorned by several carved figures, few of which remain. Originally the north-west turret was crowned by a large bartizan which was replaced in the 18th century, thereby giving the west front a symmetrical appearance.

Hylton is noteworthy for its splendid medieval heraldry. The majority of the devices are situated above the entrance, between the central turrets. Here one can see a banner bearing the arms of Henry IV (d.1413), and shields bearing the arms of Lord Lumley and many other persons of rank such as Sir Henry Percy ('Harry Hotspur,') Sir Ralph Eure and Sir William Washington. Moreover, on the southernmost of the turrets flanking the entrance, is a banner bearing the arms of Sir William de Hylton which used to be directly above the entrance. Furthermore, a large turret projecting from the east face of the castle bears the arms of Sir William Hylton and the badge of Richard II.

Upon entering, the original plan of the ground floor is easy to make out for the lower courses of the medieval partitioning walls have survived. To the north and south of a central passage were four rooms. The two rooms to the north were probably used for storage. The first room to the south was the guardroom. It controlled the entrance and housed a well. The other room seems to have accommodated one of the castle's officials.

45. The west front

An original doorway at the south-east end of the passage gives access to a newel stair in the east turret. This was the only way up from the ground floor in medieval times.

The Great Hall was located on the first floor. It was a fairly commodious room situated in a central position, with its north and south walls extending across to the west wall which they adjoined slightly to the north and south of the turrets flanking the castle's entrance. It rose to the roof and therefore was very high in comparison with its floor space. The Great Hall was the most important room in the tower-house and must have been imposing, especially when it is borne in mind that the portcullis rose into it in front of the main west window.

To the north of the Great Hall was the private apartment of the lord and his family into which they could withdraw from the communal hall. It rose two-thirds of the way to the roof. A room above - which was entered via a minor newel stair located off the north-east end of the Great Hall - possibly accommodated important guests. The space to the south of the Great Hall was occupied by four rooms, two of which were a kitchen and a buttery.

At first floor level in the east turret was a small chapel. It is no longer extant, but above it were three rooms which have survived, and all are entered via the newel stair rising from the ground floor. The first chamber probably served as the chaplain's abode. The other rooms likely accommodated officials, and both have two original windows and a hooded fireplace. The uppermost chamber is at roof-level, and had a loophole through which the battlements could be viewed. The battlements themselves had shallow troughs which could carry boiling water to the many machicolations without exposing the defenders to enemy fire.

Interestingly, an Inquisition Post Mortem drawn up after Sir William's death in 1435 states, 'there are in the same Manor a hall, four chambers, a chapel, two barns a kitchen, a house constructed of stone called the gatehouse.' The 'house' is clearly the tower-house. It has been suggested that some of the rooms referred to in the inquisition - the hall and kitchen, for example - were within the tower but it is generally accepted that they were all ancillary structures mostly ranged round a courtyard believed to have adjoined the east side of the tower-house.

In this context, the results of exploratory work undertaken at Hylton by archaeologists on 10-12 June 1994 must be mentioned. The remains of at least two buildings were located east of the tower-house. An excavation trench, 33ft by 6ft, revealed two courses of stonework associated with glazed floor tiles believed to be Flemish and contemporary with Sir William Hylton. The building of which they were part, was a high status one and it has been plausibly suggested that it may have been a banqueting hall used for ceremonial occasions, with the Great Hall in the tower-house being used for less prestigious, daily events.

The site of the other building was further east. It has been postulated that it was built several generations after the castle and faced south to enjoy commanding views of ornamental gardens evidently located on terraced ground between it and nearby Hylton Dene. The gardens are believed to have dated from the 16th or 17th century.

As has been noted, the inquisition mentions a chapel. This is no doubt a reference to the Chapel of St Catherine which stands just to the north-east of the castle and though ruined, is still largely intact. A chapel may well have occupied the site since the 12th century, but the earliest substantial extent of masonry dates from the early 15th century and is thus contemporary with the castle. On the other hand, the two-storey transepts were constructed during the Tudor era.

Hylton Castle is cared for by English Heritage, but unfortunately only the grounds are at present open to the public.

46. St Catherine's Chapel

JARROW - ST PAUL'S CHURCH

'**K**ing Egfrith, deeply impressed by the venerable Benedict's virtue, industry and devotion, and seeing that the land he had granted him for building a monastery had borne good fruit, increased his gift by the additional grant of an estate of forty hides....A year later, with King Egfrith's approval, or rather at his bidding, Benedict...built a monastery dedicated to the blessed apostle Paul...' This is how the monastic historian, Bede, (c.673-735) opens his account of the monastery of Jarrow, one of the most important centres of religion and learning founded in Anglo-Saxon England.

The key players in the event were Egfrith, who had ascended the throne of Northumbria in 671 and who was to perish in battle in 685, and a remarkable man called Benedict Biscop. The latter was born into an aristocratic family in 628 and renounced the world when twenty-five after serving as a retainer at the court of one of Egfrith's predecessors. He journeyed to Rome - the first of six such pilgrimages - and spent time at seventeen European monasteries, including the famous establishment at Lérins off the south coast of France where he took his vows. Moreover, for two years he served as abbot of the monastery of St Peter and St Paul, Canterbury.

Upon returning to Northumbria he received a generous grant of land at Wearmouth (today's Monkwearmouth) upon which to found a monastery. He did just that in 674 and as Bede notes above, the venture bore 'good fruit.' Hence in 681 Egfrith granted Biscop another substantial estate at 'In Gyrwum' (Jarrow) some seven miles to the north-west to found a sister establishment. The site was just to the south of the Tyne and on the north bank of a tributary, the little River Don, and the name 'In Gyrwum' referred to marshy terrain.

Biscop sent a small number of monks from Wearmouth to form the nucleus of the sister monastery, placing them under a trusted colleague, Ceolfrith, who was to serve as abbot. Bede describes Ceolfrith as 'industrious in everything he did, quick-minded, energetic, mature in judgement, and intensely dedicated to the religious life.' It is a description based on personal knowledge for Bede spent almost his entire life as a member of the twin monastery of Wearmouth and Jarrow.

By 685 work on the new site was sufficiently advanced for its main place of worship, the Basilica of St Paul, to be dedicated. This occurred on 23 April.

In January 690 Benedict Biscop died after a long illness, and by this date Ceolfrith was serving as abbot of both Wearmouth and Jarrow, having presumably moved to the earlier and larger monastic site. He presided over the joint foundation in an admirable manner until 716 when he resigned the abbacy in order to undertake a pilgrimage to Rome. As abbot, he had enhanced the spiritual and secular resources of the double monastery and had ensured that a high standard of monastic life was maintained.

Ceolfrith's successor as abbot of Wearmouth and Jarrow was called Hwaetbert, an individual who had a taste for writing complex poetry. It was during his abbacy that Bede died in 735. Bede is our principal source for the history of the monastery, and the record of subsequent events is not as full as could be wished.

Details of Bede's life are likewise scarce. Although he wrote copiously on a wide variety of subjects, including history, science and theology, he was reticent about himself. He tells us that he entered the monastic world at Wearmouth when aged seven, and it is usually maintained that two years later he was among those who accompanied Ceolfrith to form the nucleus of the foundation at Jarrow. Bede certainly lived at Jarrow for part of his life, and died here in 735, but the late H.L. Robson has persuasively argued that he may have been resident at Wearmouth for much longer than is usually maintained, only taking up residence at Jarrow following the commencement of Hwaetbert's abbacy.

In 793 Viking raiders entered Northumbrian waters and destroyed the monastery at Lindisfarne - the first such attack on an English monastery. The following year another Northumbrian monastery suffered the same fate. Jarrow is usually identified as the unfortunate site, but this is not certain. What is certain is this: during the course of the next century Viking raids increased and resulted in large-scale invasions by armies intent on conquest. Amid the murder and the mayhem, the fear and the destruction, monastic life was profoundly affected and most monasteries ceased to exist. Jarrow was no exception: by about 870 it was no longer extant.

During the 10th century much of England witnessed a monastic revival. The North, however, only did so in the 11th century. In the mid 1070s three monks involved in this process arrived at Jarrow after travelling north from Winchcombe. One of the monks was Aldwin, whose interest in the region had been stimulated by reading Bede. Aldwin and his colleagues set about restoring the site and were soon augmented by likeminded individuals. Work on constructing claustral monastic quarters was also undertaken, c.1076-c.1080. But in 1083 the Bishop of Durham, William of St Calais, transferred the majority of the group to Durham to form the nucleus of a Benedictine monastery he was founding. Hence Jarrow became a cell of Durham Cathedral Priory, inhabited by a master and a few monks and remained such until the Dissolution of the Monasteries in the reign of Henry VIII.

Description

The site is approached from the west and north. The dominant feature is the Church of St Paul. It is not entirely original. West of the tower, it dates from 1866 and is the work of Sir Gilbert Scott, and replaced a structure built in 1782 whose construction sadly entailed the demolition of the main monastic church - the Basilica of St Paul. On the other hand, the tower and chancel to the east are Saxon. The former nonetheless postdated the basilica, though the chancel - which originally served as a separate eastern chapel - is believed to be of Biscop's time.

The tower is of four stages, and has been attributed to the days of Aldwin. However an examination of the ground and first floors reveals that they are earlier, (the buttresses must be ignored as later additions), as can be deduced by the presence of primitive round-headed openings. It has therefore been plausibly suggested that the lower stages of the tower were built in the 8th century, or even earlier, to link the basilica to the eastern chapel. In contrast, the upper stages clearly belong to the period of restoration associated with Aldwin, who thus transformed the structure into a tower. The third stage has double windows in its north and south faces which are late Saxon in style, (vernacular traditions continued after the Conquest), while the belfry has double windows which are Norman in form and set back in rectangular panels.

The chancel, or former chapel, is long and rectangular. Its walls are of roughly squared blocks of stone, many of which betray signs of Roman tooling. The quoining is side-alternate, and at least as far as the east end is concerned, consists of much larger stones. The masonry of the east wall has signs of a wide opening which presumably gave

47. Aerial view of Jarrow from the south

access to an extension, likely a square-ended chancel. The north wall has a blocked doorway which is almost certainly original. It is tall and narrow and has a round head. The chancel has several windows, some of which are not Saxon. However, the south wall has three little round-headed windows which are Saxon and generally believed to be original. Each has jambs comprising one upright and one flat stone, and the apertures of two of the windows are partly closed by stone slabs placed flush with the outer face of the wall. It has been plausibly maintained that the builders had no glass of the right size for the windows and that the slabs were consequently used as frames. Higher up, just to the west of the westernmost of the three windows, are remnants of what is believed to have been a doorway to a gallery above the west end of the chapel.

St Paul's is now entered from the north via a porch, which though modern, houses a collection of baluster shafts and other carved stones dating from the Saxon period. The porch gives access to the north aisle - again modern - and to the south of which is the nave, likewise Scott's work. Here the most notable feature is the original dedication stone. It is now built into the west face of the tower, above a wide arched opening which gives access to the chancel. The Latin inscription reads: 'The dedication of the church of St Paul on the ninth of the kalends of May in the fifteenth year of King Egfrith and the fourth year of Ceolfrith, abbot, and with God's help the founder of this church.' It is the oldest such stone in England.

As has been stated, Scott's nave is upon the site of the original principal monastic church. The earlier structure is known to have had a west porch of two stages. Moreover, it had a nave which measured internally 68ft by 18ft, and this had four chapels or porticus along its north and south sides which were separated by solid walls and were entered via round-headed arches which formed arcades. The east end of the church consisted of a square chancel, situated just to the west of the subsequent tower.

And what of the monastic buildings? Archaeological excavations conducted intermittently at Jarrow between 1963 and 1973 revealed significant remains of a number of structures, though not the entire complex. The area between the churches and the Don to the south was evidently terraced and on the upper terrace, and approximately 39ft to the south of the places of worship, were two structures on an east-west axis. (The ground between them and the churches was occupied by the monastic cemetery). Professor Rosemary Cramp, who directed the excavations, has described the structures as 'solid Roman-looking stone buildings.'

The westernmost, (91½ft by 26ft externally), was initially divided in two by a partitioning wall, with the east room being the largest. The building had a stone slated roof, plastered internal walls, coloured and plain glass respectively in the north and south windows, and brick-faced concrete floors. It is generally believed to have been a refectory. At some point it was destroyed by fire. The east end evidently remained desolate, while a clean floor and Saxo-Norman pottery indicated further use of the west end.

The other building measured 60ft by 20ft externally. Its outer walling was covered in a plaster skin, while internally there was thick, creamy plaster. Along the south and east walls fragments of plain and coloured glass were discovered. The building contained three rooms, of which the westernmost was the largest. To the east of the partitioning wall, and evidently separated by a wooden screen, were two small rooms. The north one

48. Model of the Anglo-Saxon monastery of St Paul's, Jarrow, as
it may have appeared in the early 8th century. ©Bede's World

49. The reconstructed Anglo-Saxon farm at Bede's World, Jarrow

had an opus signinum floor and contained what may have been an altar. The other room, entered by a door in the south wall, had a sink or wash place. Of the building, Cramp has commented that it was 'a type of "cell" composed of oratory and living room...combined with a public room for communal use.'

To the south of these buildings, and lower down, were wattle huts, while nearer the river was another significant stone building which probably originally served as a guest house for visiting laity. Later it evidently was associated with glass-making.

The Department of the Environment has marked out the lines of the Saxon monastic buildings in the grass. On the other hand, substantial remains of quarters from the days of Aldwin and Jarrow's period as a cell of Durham are visible.

A short distance to the north of St Paul's is Jarrow Hall, a fine Georgian house, which contains much of interest relating to the Anglo-Saxon monastery, as does a striking new neighbouring museum constructed as part of the exciting Bede's World programme, something which has also entailed the creation on an adjoining 11 acre site of an experimental farm with timber buildings, breeds of animals, and agricultural methods, familiar in Bede's day. In short, Jarrow has been transformed into an even more fascinating site for anyone interested in Bede and his world.

KILLHOPE LEAD MINING CENTRE

The Pennines are 'the backbone of England', a chain of mountainous country stretching from the Peak District of Derbyshire to the Scottish border. A number of roads cross the Pennines and one such is the A689. Upon heading west up Weardale the road begins rising steeply and rather tortuously in the vicinity of the village of Wearhead, leading up onto the Pennines. Not long after making the ascent, one catches sight of a large water wheel and associated buildings to one's left - Killhope Lead Mining Centre.

Killhope is situated at an elevation of 1,530ft above sea level in remote and windswept upper Weardale. In the mid 19th century Weardale was the principal lead mining area in County Durham and was at the heart of the North Pennine orefield, the most productive lead producing area in Britain at a time when Britain was the world's leading producer of lead.

Lead mining was probably undertaken in Weardale in Roman times, and certainly occurred during the medieval period. But the major expansion of the industry commenced in the second half of the 17th century when there was a drive to increase production nationally in order to render the country more economically self-sufficient, thereby enhancing its competitive prospects against other nations. Fluctuations in fortune however ensued, especially during periods of war, for though conflict resulted in an increased demand for munitions this was offset by the suspension of building schemes at home and the loss of foreign markets.

From about 1820 the industry enjoyed its final boom period and one of the mines involved in this, the greatest era in the county's lead mining history, was the Park Level Mine at Killhope. It was founded in 1853 and was part of a chain of mines run by the company which dominated lead mining in Weardale, the Blackett-Beaumont Company, whose interest in lead mining in the locality dated from 1696. However, in 1883, by which time the industry had entered a period of terminal decline partly owing to cheap imports, the company pulled out of mining in Weardale and like other major mines formerly run by the company, Park Level was taken over by the newly established Weardale Lead Company.

Park Level was a 'cross-cut' mine. In other words, instead of following along the line of a vein, it intercepted veins nearly at right-angles, with workings branching off the main level to follow the veins, the nearest of which was 330ft from the mine entrance.

For over twenty years Park Level's output was nondescript. Little lead ore was extracted from the first four veins encountered. But then veins were reached which proved more productive and the workforce thus expanded to between 80 and a 100 men, significantly higher than had been the case. Furthermore, in 1876 it was decided to build a crushing mill at the mine thereby obviating the need to use a crushing plant at Burn Bottom a quarter of a mile away.

The miners worked in partnerships of usually between 4 and 6 men and were paid for the ore they produced. Where possible, they used tools such as picks to reach the lead ore, but they also employed gunpowder or dynamite (the latter was used from the 1870s), to blast away rock where necessary. It was a tough, dangerous job, and one rendered worse by frequent dampness and poor ventilation. Pumping was one of the

50. Killhope, looking south-east towards the crushing mill

methods employed to extract water - a hydraulic engine was installed in Park Level in 1867, as was a steam pump in the 1880s - while one of the methods used to improve the quality of air in the workings was to use boys to turn large fans located underground. Despite such measures, at times the quality of the air was such that mining had to be abandoned.

The method of mining undertaken was 'stoping,' whereby veins were worked out upwards. As the stoping increased in height a sturdy platform of substantial timber was constructed across the vein so that work could continue higher up the vein, and if required, the process would be repeated again at a higher level. 'Bouse', i.e., rock containing lead ore, was dropped down a chute on one side of the platform so that it could be transported out of the mine. The first stage of the journey would normally be in hand-pushed tubs, but horse drawn waggons on the main level would complete the process, taking the bouse to rows of storage bays. 'Deads' - rock not bearing lead ore and other waste material such as fluorite - was allowed to lie on the platform but in due course was either dumped in worked out parts of the mine, backfilled, or transported out of the mine in tubs and offloaded onto the dead heap beside Killhope burn which gradually washed it away.

As noted above, mining was a dangerous occupation, and the following is a record of an accident which occurred at Park Level in 1864:

'Thomas Rowell and Graham Peart were working high up in a rise when a sudden heavy fall carried Peart to his death. Rowell...though struck was able to maintain his position. The moans of his mate coming up from below soon ceased then, in Stygian darkness, the crashing of stones flying past him was the only sound he heard for three days and nights. He kept himself alive by eating his tallow candles and catching falling drops of water.'

After leaving the mine, bouse was transported to teams or rows of storage bays situated on the dressing floor near the crushing mill. The teams held the bouse of different partnerships of miners. Here the process of 'dressing,' i.e., washing and separating the bouse, commenced so that clean galena could be sent for smelting and many of those involved in the process were young boys who were expected to work long and hard in weather conditions which were often far from pleasant.

Park Level Mine ceased operating in 1916, and the site began to decay. But in 1968 the train of events which led to the establishment of Killhope Lead Mining Centre began when Durham County Council carried out minor repairs to the decaying buildings and created a picnic site. In 1980 work on restoring the crushing mill began, while in 1984 a visitors' centre was opened. The process of transforming Killhope into a vibrant reminder of the days of lead mining in Weardale has continued, with for instance work being undertaken to open part of the mine to visitors.

Description

Killhope Lead Mining Centre is situated on the south bank of Killhope Burn, and the first point of call is the Visitors' Centre which, among other things, contains an exhibition dealing with the history of Park Level Mine.

A short distance to the east of the Visitors' Centre one comes to what is known as the mineshop. The cottages of many of the men and boys who worked at Killhope were some distance from the mine and thus, as was the case at many other lead mines, some of the workforce slept at Park Level in the lodging room, which was located at the west end of the mineshop and on the first floor. This contained four bunks in which 32 people could sleep, and such overcrowding was obviously not conducive to good health. Each inmate would have brought his own food, which was cooked in the room over a peat fire. At night, working clothes were hung in front of the fire to dry off, and this added to the insalubrious conditions for harmful clouds of dust were given off as a result. This, combined with the dampness, dust and foul air experienced while in the mine, caused lung diseases. The lodging room is adjoined to the east by a room which may have served as a store room, and beyond this is an office where mine plans etc. were kept. Beneath these two rooms are the stables which served the mine's ponies, while beneath the lodging room is the smithy which contains the blacksmith's hearth, one of the few features at Killhope which has survived intact. In addition to shoeing the ponies, the blacksmith made and repaired equipment and machinery.

Just beyond the mineshop, and facing west, is the entrance to the mine. In 1996, 80 years after Park Level ceased operating, the mine was reopened and visitors can thus go underground and gain an insight into the conditions experienced by many of those who formerly worked at Killhope. It is an unforgettable experience. Before entering the mine hard hats and cap lamps are issued, as are waterproof overshoes for visitors without wellington boots. Staff then guide visitors down the tunnel, which in places is only 4ft 9in high, and has water running along the floor. A distinct drop in temperature will be noted for the mine is cool even in summer. About a 100 yards or so into Park Level several features of lead mining as practised here, and elsewhere, have been recreated just off the tunnel in an area of mock workings constructed with fibreglass. For instance, one of the displays shows a partnership working a stope. 'To fully experience a lead mine', states Killhope Centre's manager Ian Forbes, 'would mean exploring miles of tunnels and shafts - a lengthy ordeal which is neither desirable nor practical, considering the age and condition of the old workings here. But by linking the new underground chamber with the

51. The dressing floor. The entrance to the mine can be seen
immediately to the left of the building in the middle distance.

original workings we can take visitors through a very realistic scenario.'

A short distance to the east of the mine entrance lies the dressing floor. Here, as noted above, bouse which had been brought out of Park Level was dressed so that clean galena could be extracted. A variety of methods was used. However, the most important device on the dressing floor was the 'hotching tub'. This consisted of a large tub containing water and a sieve suspended from a manually operated lever which was jerked up and down, thereby moving the sieve in the water, a process which resulted in the galena (which is heavier than other minerals) forming a bottom layer on the sieve. Some ore, though, was too mixed up with other minerals such as fluorspar for it to be separated successfully on the dressing floor and was thus sent to the crushing mill to be ground into small fragments.

The mill, which is located just to the south-east of the dressing floor, is the most imposing feature at Killhope. It chiefly consists of two substantial buildings and a large water wheel 33ft 8in in diameter and 6ft wide. It was powered by water supplied from two small reservoirs on the hillside above. These were part of an extensive supply system which included other reservoirs and carried water in a series of races over a distance of up to nine miles to Killhope. Moreover the tail race of the wheel carried water down the valley to Burtree Pasture Mine and Westgate, 3 and 8 miles away respectively.

The wheel hauled bouse up an incline to the crusher rollers located between the wheel and the 'jigger house', the building adjoining to the east. An elevator then lifted the crushed bouse up the side of the building to an opening near the top where it was fed through to a series of trommels: a succession of rotating cylindrical sieves each of which had larger perforations than the one before it, so that the bouse was separated into even-sized lots. From the trommels it was fed onto 'jigs' which performed the same function as hotching tubs but were operated mechanically. They produced waste, a layer of bouse, and galena. The remaining bouse or 'middlings' went to another set of crushing rollers, this time within the jigger house, to be crushed finer and re-treated, and like all the machinery in the building this set of rollers was powered by the water wheel.

Fine bouse which was too small for jigging was carried in a stream of water in an overhead trough through the buddle house - located just to the east of the jigger house - to the classifier standing against the east side of the buddle house. The classifier was a large inverted pyramid built of stone with an opening on its top. Some of the water and very light waste was carried across the top of it. On the other hand, some water and heavier material containing lead ore sank to the bottom of the pyramid from where a pipe carried it to four buddles in the buddle house, which were driven by their own water wheel, a much smaller affair than the main wheel referred to above. The buddles have been likened to large upturned saucers. A slurry of fine bouse was fed onto the high centre of each buddle and was then distributed evenly over the whole surface by revolving brushes. While the light waste was distributed towards the edge, the ore settled nearer the middle in increasingly pure bands and was then removed after the machine was stopped.

Lead ore separated from bouse by these and other procedures, was stored on terraces or 'bingsteads' running along the front of the jigger house prior to being transported for smelting. Before 1883 the ore was carried north in horse-drawn carts to smelt mills in Allendale, but thereafter it was taken down Weardale to Rookhope Smelt Mill.

Finally, if time permits, before leaving the site one should explore a walkway provided in the woodland growing on much of the hillside to the south of the centre. It begins near the crushing mill and wends its way around to end next to the mineshop. En route it passes the two small reservoirs mentioned earlier and heads down what appears to be a natural valley - Hazely Hush. It is not. Prior to the establishment of Park Level Mine a popular method of reaching lead ore was by 'hushing,' i.e., building a small earth dam on a hillside above the line of a vein. The surface was loosened somewhat below the dam, and in due course the dam was broken, sending a torrent of water down the hillside which swept away earth and boulders. Repeated hushing created artificial valleys such as Hazely Hush, which is enchanting. The quality of the walk is enhanced by various features, such as mock mine shafts, provided by Durham County Council to serve as additional reminders of the area's lead mining past.

52. Killhope's water wheel. The wheel powered machinery in the adjoining crushing mill.

LUMLEY CASTLE

umley Castle is one of the finest castles in County Durham. It stands majestically on sloping ground to the east of the River Wear and has panoramic views westward across the river towards the historic town of Chester-le-Street nearby, and the distant Pennines beyond.

For centuries the castle was the principal residence of one of England's noblest families - the Lumleys - of whom Robert Surtees wrote: 'The family of Lumley is one of the very few whose antiquity reaches, on indisputable evidence, to the Saxon era.' It is a view to which many have subscribed, before and since, for it is claimed that the Lumleys are descended from an Anglo-Saxon nobleman called Ligulf, who played a prominent part in the affairs of the bishopric of Durham during the episcopate of Walcher of Lorraine following the Norman Conquest.

According to the traditional pedigree, Ligulf's successor, Uchtred, was in turn succeeded by a son called William, who was resident at Lumley during the episcopate of Hugh du Puiset (1153-95). But is there 'indisputable evidence' that the Lumleys are descended from Ligulf? Not according to *The Complete Peerage*, the most authoritative work of its kind. Whilst agreeing that a certain William de Lumley was resident hereabouts during the days of Puiset, it states that there is no evidence that William's father, Uchtred, 'the earliest probable ancestor of the family,' was Ligulf's son of the same name for 'there must have been one, if not two, generations between them.'

The first notable Lumley was called Ralph, and became head of the family in 1374 when aged about fourteen. He enjoyed greater wealth and standing than his predecessors, largely owing to the inheritance of estates which had belonged to some of his maternal ancestors, the Thwengs of Kilton.

In 1384 'Radulpho de Lomley' was summoned to parliament by name, where he would have sat among the lords temporal. The number of people who received individual writs of summons fluctuated from year to year, and some who were so summoned were not summoned again. But Lumley was summoned to parliament by name every year for the rest of his life, and was no doubt regarded by many of his contemporaries as a baron, and owing to his frequent summonses is held to have been the first Lord Lumley.

Surtees aptly describes Ralph as 'a man of active and enterprising spirit.' For example, he participated in the Hundred Years War and, in 1384, distinguished himself by capturing several Frenchmen whom he held for ransom. Moreover, in addition to fighting against the French, Ralph served against the Scots. In 1387-88 he served in the garrison of the important border town of Berwick-upon-Tweed and in the latter year was captured at the Battle of Otterburn, a disastrous defeat for the English.

Following his release upon the payment of a large ransom, (part of which was paid by Richard II), Ralph received permission to build a castle at Lumley, first from Bishop Walter Skirlaw in 1389, and then from Richard II in 1392, by which time he had been appointed Captain of Berwick. The castle replaced a manor house, much of which was incorporated within the west range of the new structure.

Lumley's life ended violently. In late 1399 Richard was overthrown and incarcerated by his kinsman, Henry of Lancaster, who with parliament's sanction became Henry IV.

Some of the highly unpopular deposed monarch's friends, however, plotted to restore him and Ralph was one of those party to the plan. But in January 1400 they were trapped at Cirencester by forces loyal to Henry IV, and though some managed to escape, others, including Lumley, were captured and immediately executed in the streets of the town by a vengeful mob.

Following the suppression of the rising, most of the Lumley lands were granted to the Earl of Somerset. However, in 1405 Ralph's son, John, obtained their restoration. Unlike his father, John was not summoned to parliament, but like him he did participate in the Hundred Years War and was indeed killed whilst doing so at Bauge in 1421.

John's son and successor, Thomas, was appointed Constable of Scarborough Castle in Yorkshire for life on 28 May 1455, shortly after the commencement of the Wars of the Roses. Lumley belonged to the Yorkist party, and in July 1461, not long after its great victory at Towton, he was summoned by name to Edward IV's first parliament, through which he is deemed to have become the second Baron Lumley. He was certainly referred to on a number of occasions as Lord Lumley. He later turned against Edward IV, but survived, and in due course supported the usurpation of Richard III in 1483.

The fifth baron, John, participated in the unsuccessful rising known as the Pilgrimage of Grace in 1536 during the reign of Henry VIII, as did his son, George. In the following year some die-hard opponents of the king rose again. George was one of them, and after the revolt failed he was executed on 2 June 1537.

His son, John, became head of the family in 1544 or 1545 upon the death of the fifth baron, but he did not inherit the barony owing to his father's execution as a traitor. However, an Act of Parliament of 1547 decreed that henceforth 'John Lumley, and the heirs male of his body coming, may and shall by the authority of this present parliament have...and bear the name...and pre-eminence of a Baron of this realm.'

Camden described Lord Lumley as 'a person of entire virtue.' He was a cultured individual - he was for instance a keen painter and an enthusiastic antiquary. His historical interests included a fascination with family history, a fascination which, among other things, led him to adorn Lumley Castle with shields bearing the arms of families from which he claimed descent.

In 1603 James VI of Scotland was entertained at Lumley Castle whilst travelling south following his accession to the English throne, and during the visit he was subjected to such a lengthy account of the Lumley pedigree by the Bishop of Durham that he reportedly exclaimed: 'Oh mon, gang nae further! I maun digest the knowledge I hae gained this day, for I didna ken Adam's ither name was Lumley.'

Lord Lumley died in 1609 without a son and so the barony died with with. His successor Richard, was a descendant of the second son of the fourth baron.

Richard became a peer in 1628 when Charles I created him Viscount Lumley of Waterford in the Irish peerage and during the subsequent Civil War he fought for the king and garrisoned Lumley Castle on his behalf. He died in about 1663 and was succeeded by his grandson, who was also called Richard.

In 1685 this interesting individual - who enhanced his wealth by exploiting coal reserves on his estate at Lumley - played a part in suppressing the Protestant Duke of Monmouth's rebellion, and according to the diarist John Evelyn, found the ill-fated duke hiding 'in a dry ditch covered with fern brakes.' At this date Lumley was a Catholic. However, he subsequently became a Protestant and in June 1688 was one of 'seven persons of quality' who signed a letter to William of Orange, a champion of Protestantism, inviting him to invade England and replace the unpopular Catholic monarch, James II. Following William's arrival, Lumley secured Newcastle on his behalf in

53. Lumley Castle from the south-west

December 1688, and for his part in the 'Glorious Revolution' he was created Viscount Lumley of Lumley Castle in April 1689. Then, on 15 April 1690, he was created Earl of Scarborough. He died of apoplexy at his house in Soho, on 17 December 1721.

During the days of the second earl, (who shot himself in 1740), the noted architect, Sir John Vanbrugh, who was chiefly responsible for such marvels as Castle Howard and Blenheim Palace, carried out modernization work at Lumley Castle for 'State, Beauty and Convenience.' The elderly architect did so for a sum which he said 'could never lie heavy on the family.'

Despite this, the third earl preferred to reside at Sanbeck Hall near Rotherham, which he had inherited in 1723 upon the death of his cousin, the Earl of Castleton. Subsequent heads of the family have likewise preferred to live at Sanbeck, which has become the family's principal residence. The present head of the line is Richard Aldred Lumley, twelfth Earl of Scarborough, who inherited the title in 1969. In 1993 he was one of several 'backwoodsmen', (peers who seldom attend parliament), who did so to oppose the Maastricht Bill, believing it to be against the nation's interests.

As for Lumley Castle, it is still owned by the family and is leased to a company which has transformed it into a luxury hotel.

Description

The castle is situated in pleasant parkland, and as the Victorian historian, J.R. Boyle stated, its position 'is in every way charming.' It belongs to a category of castle sometimes referred to as 'fortified houses.' Castles of this type were constructed in England from the

14th century onward with greater emphasis on domestic comfort than had been the case in previous centuries. Nonetheless, unlike say Herstmonceux in Sussex, Lumley was strongly built, no doubt in case of Scottish incursions.

In plan, the castle is almost square with a substantial courtyard surrounded by ranges of buildings, and with massive projecting four-storey towers at each corner. From east to west, it measures 196ft, whilst from north to south it is 175ft. It is reminiscent of romantic Bolton Castle in Wensleydale, Yorkshire - the work of John Lewyn - and it is by no means improbable that this distinguished architect subsequently designed Lumley Castle, for as Barrie Dobson has commented, 'he presided over the most intensive campaign of castle building seen in northern England since the 12th century.'

One approaches the castle from the west, up a tree-lined avenue. The towers of the west front, like those to the east, are imposing. At each corner they have diagonal buttresses surmounted by octagonal turrets furnished with machicolations and crenellations, whilst the parapets of the walls in between are likewise crenellated. Nonetheless,

54. The west front

the west front is not forbidding. This is due to Vanbrugh, for he transformed the west front into the principal facade by constructing the stairs and terrace (between the west towers), which give access to the simple front door - also Vanbrugh's work - located in the centre of the west range. The sash windows here, and elsewhere at Lumley for that matter, likewise date from this time, as do the five oval windows above them and the cupola adorning the roof.

In contrast, the east front retains much of its medieval character, and here one finds the original entranceway. The decision to have the entrance here is immediately intelligible, for a few yards to the east the ground falls away precipitously to form the heavily wooded ravine of the Lumley Beck; a daunting natural obstacle for would-be assailants.

The gatehouse is flanked by tall, square turrets with machicolated parapets. Between the turrets are additional machicolations, beneath which are six heraldic shields located directly above the entrance. One bears the arms of Ralph Lumley - a fesse between three popinjays - whilst the others bear the arms of families connected to the Lumleys such as the Percies, Nevilles and Hyltons.

Upon walking through the entrance one comes to the courtyard. This measures 76ft from east to west, and 73ft from north to south, and retains much of its medieval atmosphere, despite the fact that Vanbrugh constructed a stately corridor along the north front of the south range, (thereby linking the east and west ranges).

Directly opposite the gatehouse is a gateway which was formerly the entrance of the manor house which preceded the castle. It originally gave access to a no longer extant courtyard directly to the west of the west range. The gateway is flanked by semi-octagonal turrets, whilst above the ent-rance (with its two arches and a portcullis in between), are eighteen shields arrayed in two vertical col umns which were placed here by John, Lord Lumley, in Elizabethan times.

Directly above the passage of the gateway is the Baron's Hall, situated on the first floor. Formerly the Great Hall, it

55. A 19th century engraving of the east front

measures 58½ft from north to south, and is just under 31ft wide. The room contains a large fireplace dating from Elizabethan times: it has Roman Doric columns, guilloche decoration and, upon the overmantel, a shield bearing the arms of the Lumleys and related families such as the FitzAlans. The Baron's Hall is the setting for 'Elizabethan' banquets when up to 200 revellers at a time feast here beneath overhangings, and with entertainers in period costume providing songs and mirth.

On the first floor of the north-west tower is the kitchen, which occupies two storeys. It has three fireplaces (two of them over 12ft wide), and an external flight of steps which gives access to an 18th century service courtyard to the north.

On the first floor of the south-west tower is the Garter Room, the most impressive of the State Rooms. It measures 52ft (from east to west) by 27ft, and its walls and coved ceiling with imitation coffering are decorated with superb plasterwork - generally believed to be the work of Pietro Francini - which was executed in the 1740s for the third Earl of Scarborough. The room is so named because its ceiling has a panel with the Garter Star in its centre in honour of the second Earl of Scarborough, K.G.

Below, is Vanbrugh's Library. Originally, there were no living-rooms at ground floor level, but Vanbrugh transformed the vaulted undercroft here into this unusual room with its three groin-vaulted aisles, stone fireplace, and boldly rusticated piers.

On the first floor of the south range are the Waterford Room and the Vanbrugh Bar. The former adjoins the Garter Room and is subdued and elegant, with fine panelling and a simple plaster ceiling.

In the south-east tower, and also on the first floor, is the Scarborough Room, with a Rococo ceiling and a two-light Perpendicular east window being of interest. To the north, in the east range, is the Sandbeck Room, which likewise has a Rococo ceiling.

And what of the north-east tower? Its tunnel-vaulted undercroft is used as the hotel reception. Originally, the first floor was occupied by the chapel, but it has been divided into bedrooms. The floor above has three cinquefoil-headed windows, whilst the top floor retains its original fireplace and windows. Finally, there are no rooms of conse-quence in the north range.

MONKWEARMOUTH, ST PETER'S CHURCH

'Christ's devout servant Benedict Biscop, inspired by divine grace, built a monastery in honour of Peter, the most blessed chief of the apostles, at the mouth of the River Wear on its north bank.' These words by Bede refer to one of the most significant events in the history of English monasticism - the foundation of the monastery of Monkwearmouth in 674.

As noted in the chapter on St Paul's, Jarrow, the monastery was founded by a Northumbrian nobleman, Benedict Biscop, who had experienced life in many continental monasteries and had briefly served as the abbot of the monastery of St Peter and St Paul, Canterbury, before returned to his homeland to found a monastery of his own.

Upon doing so, Biscop approached the king, Egfrith, and Bede relates that the monarch was so moved by what he heard that he granted Biscop a considerable estate at *Wiuraemuda* - Monkwearmouth - upon which to found such an establishment.

Within barely a year of the monastery's foundation, Biscop again made his way across to Gaul to secure the services of skilled workmen who could build him a stone church 'in the Roman style' which he loved. His desire to build such a church necessitated the hiring of foreign craftsmen, and they were soon joined by glaziers who were also brought across from Gaul because the Anglo-Saxons were unfamiliar with glazing windows.

Once the construction work was completed Biscop set about turning the monastery into a seat of learning, for he wished to promote scholarship and was himself a skilled theologian versed in Latin and Greek. He had already acquired an impressive collection of books during his travels abroad and during two further visits to Rome (in 678-9 and 684-7), he obtained additional copies. Through such efforts he founded an 'immense library of books on every branch of learning' and it was primarily through use of this monastic library that Bede himself acquired his considerable learning.

Benedict Biscop died after a long illness on 12 January 690. One of his last requests was that the magnificent

56. St Peter's Church from the west

library he had acquired be preserved in its entirety for the use of future generations. This was totally in character, for Biscop's place in history chiefly rests on the very important part he played in the advancement of learning. Of his achievements in general, the late Sir Frank Stenton has observed, he 'brought into being two neighbouring monasteries, governed as a single community, which possessed an endowment in relics, religious ornaments, and books unparalleled in England.'

Life in the monastery was governed by a Rule devised by Biscop. This was based on his experience of life in other monasteries and, more particularly, on the Rule of the famous 6th century Italian abbot, St Benedict, which enjoined upon those who vowed to obey it, a self-sacrificing life devoted to the service of God. At regular intervals day and night, the monks would have gathered to observe the Canonical hours. The time in between would have been largely devoted to activities such as studying the Bible and providing for the needs of the community. The latter necessitated manual labour such as ploughing, and Bede relates that among those who engaged in such work was Biscop's kinsman, Eosterwin, who was in charge at Monkwearmouth during Bede's absence in the mid 680s and died of plague in 686. Of him, Bede wrote: 'This amiable man was born of noble parentage, but did not allow the privileges of birth to infect his heart with the ordinary passions of the great, vanity, ostentation, pride, and a spirit of disdain for inferiors.'

At the time of Biscop's death the monastery was under the control of another admirable individual, Ceolfrith, who was to hold the abbacy until 716 when he retired to conduct a pilgrimage to Rome. He took with him one of three copies of Jerome's Vulgate translation of the Bible which had been transcribed by monks under his charge, with the intention of presenting it to the Pope. Sadly, he died en route at Langres in Burgundy, but the copy of the Bible was taken to Rome by some of the monks who had accompanied him. It is now in the Laurenziana Library, Florence, and is known as the *Codex Amiatinus*. It is a work of tremendous importance for it is one of the oldest and finest transcriptions of the Vulgate in existence. It not only highlights the skill and assiduity of the monks who worked in the scriptorium of Monkwearmouth/Jarrow, but also testifies to the monastery's wealth, for it has been estimated that 1,550 calves were slaughtered to provide the vellum for the codex and its companion volumes.

During the latter half of the 9th century, large-scale Viking invasions of England resulted in the general cessation of monastic life and Monkwearmouth was evidently one of the houses which ceased to exist. At the close of the 10th century Bishop Aldhun of Durham sent a small party of secular clergy here and they no doubt restored St Peter's Church. Another period of restoration occurred in the 1070s following the destruction of the site in 1070 by the Scottish king, Malcolm Canmore, while ravaging the North East coast. The work was carried out by a small group of monks who had travelled north and were intent on the revival of monasticism in the region.

However, in 1083 Bishop William of St Calais transferred the majority of them to Durham where he was founding a Benedictine priory. Monkwearmouth thus became a cell of that house. It was presided over by a master who seldom had more than a couple of monks under his charge, and on occasion the peace of the cell was disrupted by conflict with the local baronial Hylton family over such matters as non-attendance by the Hyltons of St Peter's Church for the major Church festivals such as Christmas. Indeed, following one clash in 1439 the master of Monkwearmouth, William Lyam, had to be transferred to another cell because he dared 'noght abide in his plas [Monkwearmouth] for fere of bodely harme.' The cell was dissolved in 1536 during the Dissolution of the Monasteries, but St Peter's remained to serve the needs of the parish.

Increasing use of the River Wear by colliers from the late 16th century onward led to large quantities of ballast being dumped in the vicinity of the church. So much so that in time it was partly buried. But between 1866-74 interest in the historic building resulted in the removal of the offending ballast and large-scale restoration work occurred. Moreover, the church was enlarged to meet the needs of an expanding population.

57. St Peter's in the 1780s.

Regrettably, St Peter's was deliberately set alight soon after 3 p.m. on Monday 19 March 1984 and despite the prompt arrival of emergency services, the fire (one of several started in historic churches in the region during this period), did serious damage. A programme of restoration ensued, and took at least four years to complete.

Description

The main approach is from the west. The topography has changed greatly since the days of Biscop owing to the deposition of ballast. St Peter's thus stands in a shallow hollow, whereas originally it stood on a small hill.

The most striking feature of the exterior is the tower. This is 59ft high, of five stages, and incorporates an earlier porch. More than one interpretation of its development has been given. Neither the tower, nor the porch upon which it is built, dates from the period of the church's construction for they are not bonded into the west wall of the nave. However it is clear that a west porch was soon erected for Eosterwin was buried in it. Some years later, the porch was transformed by the addition of a second storey and flanking two-storey porticus to the north and south. The porticus, which are no longer extant, were subsequently reduced to one storey, and the porch was built upon in order to form a tower. This is generally said to have occurred c.1000 when secular clergy were resident at Monkwearmouth. However, Eric Cambridge has persuasively argued recently that the tower is post-Conquest and has dated it to the late 11th century. It therefore seems most likely that it was constructed c.1080, i.e. when Aldwin and his companions were resident here.

The west entrance of the porch (which has never had a door), has a round arch of nine carefully cut voussoirs which vary in size but are all through-stones. The imposts are supported by pairs of richly ornamented baluster shafts, and the stones upon which the baluster shafts themselves rest are also ornamented. They have been carved to show (on each jamb), two interlaced creatures with beak-like jaws and fish-tails, though these are now unfortunately very badly worn.

The side doorways, which gave access from the porch to the porticus, both have jambs, imposts, and a round arch all of through-stones, as does the porch's east doorway. The latter evidently replaced an earlier opening which was taller and offset slightly to the south, and probably dates from when the porticus were constructed - likely during the abbacy of Ceolfrith - owing to its similarity to the lateral doorways.

The porch has a barrel-vault. This no doubt dates from when the tower was added, for the floor of the first storey room it supports is obviously higher than it was originally. This can be determined, for example, by the blocked doorway in the north wall of the porch which is partly below the present floor-level.

The exterior of the tower's third stage has some interesting features. In the centre of the west face one can see the remains of what was a life-sized statue, perhaps a representation of St Peter. Moreover, on either side of the former statue the junction between the gable of the porch and the subsequent tower can be clearly seen. The walling of the latter generally consists of larger and more carefully dressed stones

58. The Anglo-Saxon porch: note the carved baluster shafts

than those of the earlier work, though the quoining (mainly side-alternate), is of stones smaller than those of the quoining beneath.

The uppermost stage of the tower has a double belfry window in its north, south, and west faces, each of which has a plain mid-wall shaft and a long lintel in which the round heads of the lights have been cut. They are, moreover, outlined by arched stripwork.

The west wall of the nave is 2ft thick, and like the porch, is of rubble. It is all that remains of the church's original fabric. The north quoins are predominantly large stones generally laid in side-alternate fashion, while the south quoins are smaller and clearly date from the Victorian period of restoration.

St Peter's is entered from the north - the west entrance is barred by railings - and upon crossing the north aisle constructed in the mid-1870s, one enters the nave. With the exception of the west wall, which is of course original, the nave is undoubtedly built upon the foundations of Biscop's church, which was thus 64ft long and 18ft 6in wide. The height of the nave - it is just over 30ft to the springing of the gable - was obviously determined by the survival of the west wall and this great contrast between the height and breadth of the nave is generally attributed to Frankish influence.

Three original windows can be seen in the west wall. One allowed occupants of the porch's first floor chamber to look into the church. The other windows are higher and no doubt served to light an upper storey of the church mentioned by Bede.

We know that the interior of St Peter's was once adorned by paintings which Benedict Biscop had brought from Rome. 'His intention', Bede states, 'was that all who entered the church, even those unable to read, might gaze wherever they looked upon the sight, ever dear, of Christ and His saints, if only in picture; might reflect more attentively on the blessing of the Lord's incarnation; and by having before their eyes the fateful scene of the Last Judgement might remember to examine themselves more strictly.'

It is interesting to note that the present chancel is evidently situated upon the site of the former church of St Mary (built before 684), one of two lesser churches known to have also served the monastic community. The chancel contains a tomb bearing the mutilated effigy of a member of the Hylton family which is generally believed to be that of Sir William Hylton (d.1435), the builder of Hylton Castle, located a few miles upstream from Monkwearmouth.

And what of the monastic buildings? These were to the south of St Peter's. At earlier Northumbrian monasteries such as Lindisfarne, which unlike Monkwearmouth were based on the Celtic model, the monks lived in individual cells clustered about the place of worship. At Monkwearmouth, however, while there were separate rooms for the abbot, senior monks and important guests, the majority of the community slept in a 'common dormitory.'

Excavations carried out intermittently at Monkwearmouth between 1959 and 1974 under the direction of Professor Rosemary Cramp of the University of Durham, revealed that the scale of building was extensive, and the overall standard of the monastic buildings excavated was high. Cramp has written: 'The importance of this site is that it has produced buildings regularly aligned on the church, in which the quality of construction is reminiscent of Roman work. The painted plaster, decorative stone-carving, and coloured window-glass associated with them, all indicate the reintroduction of an advanced stone technology into the area.'

Although little of Benedict Biscop's monastery has survived, Monkwearmouth is nevertheless a very important part of our heritage. It was one of the first monasteries in England, and at its height, one of the richest and most influential, and in addition to the surviving fabric, visitors to St Peter's can see a number of exhibits which will remind them of the dedication, religious enthusiasm, and artistic ability of the monks who lived and worshipped here more than a millennium ago.

RABY CASTLE

I n the early 16th century John Leland visited Raby Castle and found it to be 'the largest castel of logginges in al the north cuntery.' Raby is now larger than it was at this date. Nonetheless, in Leland's day it was still one of the most impressive castles in the north of England, surpassed in size in County Durham only by Barnard Castle and Durham Castle, and its domestic accommodation was undoubtedly generous.

Raby is situated in pleasant parkland about a mile to the north of the village of Staindrop in south-east Durham. The site is one of some antiquity - the estate once belonged to King Cnut (1016-35) - but Raby is chiefly associated with the great baronial family of Neville, two of whose members were responsible for the construction of the castle in the 14th century.

The first member of the line, Gilbert de Neville, is recorded as holding land in Lincolnshire in 1086 and that county remained the centre of the family's affairs for several generations. A subsequent head of the line, Henry, is known to have been in possession of property in Lincolnshire, Yorkshire and County Durham in the reign of King John, (1199-1216). His sister and heir, Isabel, married a Durham landowner, Robert FitzMaldred, lord of Raby, and a son of the match, Geoffrey, assumed the name of Neville though he continued to use his paternal arms of a saltire.

Geoffrey's son and successor, Robert, supported Henry III during the Barons' War, a

59. Aerial view of Raby Castle from the south

civil war fought in the 1260s, as did the majority of Durham's landowners. He was predeceased by his son and was thus succeeded in 1282 by his grandson, Ranulf.

Ranulf received repeated summonses to parliament from 1295 to 1331. He was the first of the line to receive such summonses and through them is deemed to have become the first Lord Neville of Raby. Overall, the record of his life is a conventional one, though it is interesting to note that in 1313 he was convicted of committing incest with his married daughter, Anastase.

Ranulf's eldest son, Robert, an apparently turbulent figure known as the 'Peacock of the North' on account of the magnificence of his dress, was killed on a raid against the Scots in 1319 and so in 1331 Ranulf was succeeded by another son, Ralph.

Ralph was at least forty at this time and was serving as the steward of the royal household, a position he retained until 1337. The second baron - he is sometimes erroneously referred to as the fourth Lord Neville of Raby - is best remembered for his military exploits in the year 1346. England's king, Edward III, had crossed to France earlier in the year to wage war against the forces of Philip VI but before doing so, had placed the Archbishop of York, and two senior northern barons, one of whom was Neville, in charge of defending England in case of a Scottish invasion. It proved a sensible precaution. Scotland's young king, David II, being 'stout and right jolly, and desirous to see fighting' according to the Scottish chronicler Andrew Wyntoun, crossed the border at the head of a formidable army and encamped at Beaurepaire just to the north-west of Durham City. On 17th October he was defeated in battle nearby at Neville's Cross and Ralph Neville, described as 'strong, truthful, cautious and brave, much to be feared,' in the *Lanercost Chronicle*, was in overall command of the victorious army. Ralph died on 5 August 1367 and was buried in Durham Cathedral, the first layman to be accorded such an honour.

Evidently, he was chiefly responsible for constructing Raby Castle. A consideration of architectural features indicates that the process of transforming the then seat, a manor-house, into a castle was underway in the 1340s and 1350s, with the stimulus for such activity presumably being the major Scottish incursion of 1346.

John, Ralph's son and successor - who made a number of major additions to the castle - was likewise a martial figure. For instance, he fought at Neville's Cross and was made a Knight of the Garter in 1369. He was, moreover, one of the members of Edward III's administration accused of malpractice in the Good Parliament of 1376 and though the case against him appears to have been weak, was dismissed from office. Nonetheless his fortunes soon improved, and he served as Governor of Aquitaine in 1378-81.

In 1388 the third baron was succeeded by his son, Ralph, who was created Earl of Westmorland by Richard II in 1397. Two years later, however, despite this and significant grants from the king, Ralph was a leading figure in the movement which brought about Richard's overthrow in favour of Henry of Lancaster. Neville was duly rewarded by Henry IV for his services. He was, among other things, made a Knight of the Garter and Earl Marshal of England. He married twice. His second wife, Joan, was an illegitimate daughter of John of Gaunt, the fourth son of Edward III, and upon Neville's death in 1425 the bulk of his very substantial property, which included castles elsewhere such as at Middleham in Yorkshire, was left to Joan and ultimately passed from her to the younger branch of the family. Hence the second Earl of Westmorland, (a grandson of Ralph by his first wife), entered into a denuded inheritance which chiefly comprised the castle and lordship of Brancepeth in County Durham: Raby was among the property which passed to the junior line. Not surprisingly, the senior branch of the Nevilles resented this turn of events. Indeed the second earl engaged in a desultory private war with his half-brother, Richard, (Joan's eldest son) for several years. Finally, in 1443 an agreement was reached in which

60. The east front

Westmorland agreed to recognize his half-brother's claim to the bulk of the first earl's former possessions. In return, Richard abandoned, at a price, all claims to the Neville inheritance in County Durham and thus Raby was secured for the senior line.

Raby remained in Neville hands until the reign of Queen Elizabeth when, in 1569, Charles, the sixth Earl of Westmorland, who was a devout Roman Catholic, was one of the leaders of the rebellion known as the Rising of the North. The revolt was conducted with singular incapacity and collapsed, whereupon Westmorland fled to Scotland and thence to Flanders where he died in poverty in 1601.

Westmorland's possessions were forfeited to the Crown and Raby remained in royal hands until 1626 when it was acquired by Sir Henry Vane the Elder, the son of a Kentish landowner. During the Civil Wars of the 1640s Henry supported parliament and Raby was besieged by Royalists in 1648, but suffered little damage. He was, however, opposed to the king's subsequent execution. Vane died in Kent in 1654.

His son and successor, Sir Henry Vane the Younger, was born in 1613. He studied at the Universities of Oxford, Leyden and Geneva and then spent time in New England where he served as Governor of Massachusetts in 1636-7. He soon returned to England and was elected to parliament in 1639. Though a prominent opponent of the king, he did not participate in the trial of Charles, and like his father was opposed to his execution. He retired from parliament in 1653 and because he refused to accept Cromwell as both the head of state and the army was imprisoned for a while on the Isle of Wight in 1656. Following Cromwell's death in 1658 Vane returned to parliament. Upon the Restoration of the monarchy in 1660 he was imprisoned again, for his republican principles were considered seditious. He was confined in the Tower of London and on the Isles of Scilly. He was then executed with the sanction of Charles II in 1662 for his former opposition to

Charles I and the diarist Samuel Pepys noted that he 'changed not his colour or his speech to the last, but died justifying himself and the cause he had stood for...with all humility and gravity.'

One of Vane's sons and successors, Christopher, was raised to the peerage as the first Baron Barnard by William III in 1698. The family's principal seat was still in Kent. Raby was entailed on Lord Barnard's heir, Gilbert. However, the latter's marriage angered his parents and consequently they began dismantling the castle, but they were ordered to desist and to make restitution following legal action. Gilbert became the second baron in 1723 and during his period as head of the family a programme of restoration at Raby began. Under the guidance of the architect, James Paine, significant changes were made to the castle while a highly gifted County Durham man, Thomas Wright, whose interests included a fascination with science (he wrote an important treatise on the nature of the universe) was commissioned to landscape the grounds.

Lord Barnard died in 1753. His son, Henry, was created Earl of Darlington the following year. The next head of the family, the second earl, planted many of the woods around Raby and made significant changes to the castle after engaging the services of John Carr in 1768.

The third earl, who succeeded to the title in 1792, played a key role in bringing about the Reform Act of 1832 and was created Duke of Cleveland the following year for his services. The dukedom subsequently passed to his three sons, the first of whom engaged William Burn to work at Raby in 1843. Alterations and additions were made during the course of the next decade, particularly to the south front. Upon the death of the fourth duke in 1891 the earldom of Darlington and the dukedom of Cleveland became extinct. Raby, and the title Lord Barnard, passed to Henry de Vere a descendant of the second Lord Barnard. The present Lord Barnard, the eleventh baron, is a descendant of the Nevilles of Raby through his paternal grandmother, the daughter of the third Marquess of Exeter.

Description

On 10 May 1378 Bishop Thomas Hatfield of Durham granted the third Lord Neville of Raby permission to make a castle of his manor at Raby. It would be natural to assume that the licence resulted in the construction of the castle, but as Malcolm Hislop has commented, 'the architectural evidence suggests that [the licence] marked not the beginning of the conversion from a previously undefended manor house [apparently dating from the late 13th or early 14th centuries] but the enlargement and strengthening of a castle that had been in existence for over twenty years,' additional work which John Hervey has attributed to none other than the celebrated architect, John Lewyn.

The castle is approached from the north. Despite the alterations and additions of recent centuries, it is essentially medieval and belongs to the quadrangular school of castle building.

The outer gatehouse is approached over a moat which was drained in the 18th century. It is not an imposing structure (it was reduced in height and remodelled by John Carr in 1770) and above the entrance, and running between two turrets, is a machicolated parapet. The parapets of the turrets are unusual for they are flush with the fronts of the turrets but machicolated to the sides.

A low crenellated wall running from the gatehouse encloses the castle. Originally it was much higher, providing an impressive curtain wall which, like the gatehouse, was probably constructed following the licence of 1378.

Upon walking through the gatehouse one is confronted by Clifford's Tower, an imposing structure 79ft high and with walls nearly 10ft thick, the largest in the castle. It was evidently likewise built by the third Lord Neville of Raby and rendered any assailants' approach from the gatehouse to the Neville Gateway, (to the south), difficult. Clifford's Tower has three original square-headed windows with trefoil cusping and sunken spandrels, (the other windows, though of 14th century appearance, date from c.1870, as do many of the other 14th century-style windows at Raby, some of which are indeed early 20th century.

Clifford's Tower is adjoined by the contemporaneous north-west range which connects it with an earlier tower, the Watch Tower, to the south. The Watch Tower is at the north end of the west range, roughly in the centre of which stands the projecting Neville Gateway, another addition of John Lord Neville. In large part, this is also true of Joan's Tower beyond, which boldly projects westward at the west end of the south range. Moreover, if one continues walking around the exterior, and thus passes the south front, which is the least medieval, having been extensively altered in the 18th and 19th centuries, another tower will be noted at the south-east corner of the castle. This is the five-sided Bulmer's Tower. Its date of construction is uncertain, but it most likely can be associated with the licence of 1378. Almost all the rest of the fabric dates from the days of the second Baron Neville of Raby.

The Neville Gateway gives access to the heart of the castle and is impressive. It is 62ft high, projects from the west range, and has two obliquely-placed square towers. Above the entrance arch is a machicolated parapet while higher up, and below another machico lated parapet, are three shields which enable the gatehouse to be dated to between 1381-88. The gateway was built in front of an earlier one and this has resulted in an unusually long gate passage which gives access through the range to the main court-

61. The Neville Gateway, with the Watch Tower and Joan's Tower to the left and right

yard to the east. The vaulting styles of the two gateways are in marked contrast. The later work comprises a tunnel-vault with liernes which are supported by slender colonnettes with crenellated capitals. Beyond, one finds less delicate work: a tunnel-vault with massive segmental transverse arches.

The main courtyard is roughly square in plan (to the north, and not entered by visitors, is a smaller irregular courtyard with Clifford's Tower at its northern apex). On the east side of the main courtyard is the two storey hall range, part of whose ground floor belonged to the manor-house transformed into a castle in the 14th century. The windows at this level had two trefoil-headed lights and geometrical tracery, and were comparable to the existing ones which date from the 18th century. Above, the Baron's Hall has original paired lancets with transoms and Perpendicular tracery which is among the earliest in County Durham.

Visitors begin their examination of the interior by walking along a passage in the west range which leads to a mid 18th century lobby in the south range by James Paine and Daniel Garrett. From the lobby one enters the Small Drawing Room. Though restored by both James Paine and John Carr, it was greatly altered in about 1820, perhaps by Joseph Browne. It is a comfortable

62. The east range from the courtyard

room which retains its elegant 18th century plaster ceiling with musical instruments as motifs, and contains a very fine collection of sporting and equestrian pictures, including works by John Wootton and Francis Sartorius. Among the furniture is a fine walnut bookcase of c.1710, a very early example of its type.

Progressing eastward, one enters the Library. This was originally a long medieval room but was divided into two rooms by Sir Henry Vane the Elder who employed Inigo Jones to work at Raby. The partition wall was then removed by Paine and green pilasters stand where the wall stood. The room functioned for many years as a dining room and became a library when William Burn built the present Dining Room (towards the east end of the south range) in the 1840s. It then became a drawing room - a function it has retained - but is nonetheless still known as the Library. It has a rather sombre atmosphere - wood panelling is chiefly responsible for this - and contains a number of paintings, including a portrait of Nell Gwynn by Sir Peter Lely. Also of interest, are two very tall 18th century Chinese porcelain pagodas.

The Library is adjoined by the Ante-Library, which contains some of the finest paintings at Raby, including two Dutch interiors by Pieter de Hooch, a harbour scene attributed to Claude, and works by David Teniers the Younger. The room also contains a very fine mid 17th century North Italian inlaid writing cabinet known as the 'Temple of Hymen'.

Next comes the sumptuous Octagon Drawing Room, which was modelled in 1848 by

Burn from an existing circular room. The walls are hung with yellow silk brocade, the curtains and swags are of crimson and gold silk, while the elaborately moulded and gilded ceiling has both Jacobean and Rococo motifs. Sunlight has damaged much of the textiles - which have been described by the Royal Albert Museum as astonishing both in terms of quality and quantity - and a programme of restoration thus commenced in 1993. For instance, some of the damaged silks were conserved by Caroline Rendell, while replacement silks for those too damaged were woven by the Humphries Weaving Company on the only 19th century handlooms still in commercial use in the country. The programme of restoration has also entailed reassembling the suite of gilded furniture originally supplied for the room (items had become dispersed throughout the castle), and covering it with red and gold silk to match the curtains, a task which is still underway.

From the Octagon Drawing Room one enters the Dining Room, again by Burn, but a more restrained, elegant chamber, where the predominant colour is a deep red and where most of the furniture is of mahogany. When fully extended the dining table can seat forty people. Among the paintings is a portrait of the poet Alexander Pope by Sir Godfrey Kneller, and one by Sir Joshua Reynolds of a young lady who later married the third Earl of Darlington.

From the Dining Room a passage leads indirectly northward to the Entrance or Lower Hall which has a north-south axis. Here one is located in the core of the medieval castle, though the Entrance Hall itself only dates from the 1780s when Carr remodelled this part of Raby for the second Earl of Darlington. Immediately to the west of the Entrance Hall is the main courtyard referred to above. Turning carriages in the courtyard was difficult and so Carr designed the Entrance Hall so that they could pass right through it from the courtyard and continue via a passageway, thereby emerging on the east side of the castle, something which entailed the demolition of a barbican there. The Entrance Hall is aisled and has octagonal piers faced with imitation marble which support graceful Gothic vaulting. The hall contains various items, including a collection of arms and armour and one of stuffed animals and birds. For many years visitors have also been able to see the 'Greek Slave,' a marble chained female nude sculpted by Hiram Powers which was displayed at the Great Exhibition in 1851 where it caused a sensation. It was bought by the second Duke of Cleveland in 1861. It was originally displayed in the Octagon Drawing Room and when the programme of restoration there is completed it will be returned to the room.

From the south end of the Lower Hall stairs lead to two bedrooms. First comes the Servant's Bedroom, which is furnished as it would have appeared c.1900. Another flight of stairs ascends to the Blue Bedroom, where most of the furniture dates from the 19th century, though a number of paintings are significantly earlier, such as a portrait of a judge by Van Dyke.

At the same level is the Baron's Hall. It is located above the Entrance Hall and the Octagon Drawing Room, and is the most imposing room at Raby. Some significant changes have occurred since medieval times. For instance, creating Carr's Entrance Hall necessitated raising the floor level of the Baron's Hall by about 10ft. Moreover, the hall is longer than was initially the case for in the 1840s Burn extended it southward 56ft over the Octagon Drawing Room, thereby lengthening it from 80ft to 132ft. Furthermore, he replaced the hammerbeam roof with the present beamed ceiling ornamented with bosses. There is a substantial collection of portraits from different periods, while the bulk of the furniture is Georgian or Victorian. A special feature of interest is the stone minstrels' gallery at the north end of the hall which dates from the 14th century. In 1864 its central section was removed to allow the insertion of a doorway to an imposing stair-case beyond, which was completed in that year to give access to the Baron's Hall from the north end of the Entrance Hall. The stairs are not used by visitors.

From near the north end of the Baron's Hall one progresses eastward to a chapel on the first floor of the Chapel Tower. The chapel has been dated to the 1360s, but Malcolm Hislop has recently argued that it dates from the 1340s owing to its affinities, such as 'near identical reticulated tracery', to the south aisle of nearby St Mary's Church at Stain-drop where Ralph, second Lord Neville of Raby, obtained licence to found three chantries in 1343. The chapel has experienced both neglect and restoration, (the last major phase of restoration was undertaken in 1901), and was used for the marriage of Lord Barnard's second daughter, Elizabeth, in January 1982.

On leaving the chapel, one descends to the kitchen, located in a tower on the north side of the Entrance Hall. The kitchen is a remarkable room, 30ft square and 40ft high, and the most genuinely medieval at Raby. Among other things, it has windows on three sides which are set well above floor level and are linked by a mural passage reached via stairs in the south-west corner of the kitchen. Archers could thus have been deployed at the windows in times of emergency. The kitchen's vaulted ceiling supports a ventilation lantern which provided a strong updraught, thereby removing smoke and fumes.

63. The Baron's Hall

From the kitchen, passages lead westward to the Servants' Hall, located on the ground floor of the north-west range, i.e., between the Watch Tower and Clifford's Tower. It is a long, low, vaulted room, which on its east side overlooks the lesser of Raby's two court-yards, and is believed to have originally served as the guardroom, while during the Civil Wars it was used as accommodation by the garrison. Upon leaving the Servants' Hall one soon emerges in the main courtyard, having completed the tour of the castle.

Visitors are allowed to stroll around Raby Park, which is 250 acres in extent and contains over 30 types of tree - though Beech trees are the most numerous - and is also home to two herds of deer, Red and Fallow, both of which contain descendants of deer maintained in the area since the Norman period. One can also enjoy fine gardens located a short distance to the north-west of the castle which date from the mid 18th century.

Finally, just to the north of the Gardens are the Coach Yard and Coach Houses. The latter were designed by Carr in the mid 1770s and principally house an interesting collection of 18th and 19th century coaches.

64. Raby Castle from the south-east across the park

RYHOPE PUMPING STATION

At the 1887 annual meeting of the shareholders of the Sunderland and South Shields Water Company the assembled directors and shareholders heard a ringing endorsement of the quality of the water it supplied. Mrs Ormiston Chant of the British Women's Temperance Association was quoted as saying: 'In all her ten years water drinking she had never tasted such delicious water as the water in Sunderland. Those who preferred intoxicants to it were simply idiotic.'

The Sunderland and South Shields Water Company was a flourishing concern which was to become one of the foremost private water companies in Britain, with pumping stations stretching from Cleadon in the north of County Durham as far as New Winning in the south of the county. In all, the company eventually had fifteen pumping stations extracting water from the magnesian limestone which underlies much of eastern Durham. In 1887 most of these had yet to be built, but among those which were in existence was Ryhope Pumping Station which had been constructed within twenty years of the company's foundation in 1852.

The company was founded through the merger of the Sunderland Water Company with that of neighbouring South Shields. The former was not the first such company which operated on Wearside. That honour belonged to the Bishopwearmouth Water Company founded in 1824, which had a well 162ft deep in Waterworks Road. A government report of 1845 (by which time Bishopwearmouth had become part of Sunderland), notes that the Bishopwearmouth Water Company supplied piped water to 670 houses out of a total of 6,086 in Sunderland, and that its 29 standpipes supplied its 'pure and good' water to many less fortunate individuals. The report contains different opinions about the quality of the company's operations. For one thing, it was censured by some for its practice of turning off the mains at night, and from Saturday night until Monday morning.

Such criticism led the Council to seek parliamentary sanction for the establishment of another water company. Despite opposition from the supporters of the established company, this was forthcoming and so in 1846 the Sunderland Water Company was founded. It immediately set to work constructing a pumping station on Humbledon Hill and, in early 1847, took over the Bishopwearmouth Water Company. Its growth was rapid. 'Within two years of foundation,' states H.J. Smith, its income 'was almost double that of the old company', and in 1852 it successfully sought parliamentary sanction to merge with the South Shields Water Company (which had come into existence in 1788), and thus the Sunderland and South Shields Water Company was created.

In 1852 a new pumping station was established at Fulwell (then a village a short distance to the north of Sunderland), and in 1862 work on another station, at nearby Cleadon, likewise commenced. Such was the demand for water from the growing town of Sunderland that the company was also considering the establishment of a pumping station at Ryhope, a couple of miles to the south of the town. In 1860 it had tried to purchase land at Ryhope for this purpose but was put off by the asking price. However, in 1863 the company's engineer, Thomas Hawksley, a man of national reputation and likely the finest waterworks engineer of the century, persuaded the directors to reopen negotiations for the four acre site. The land was consequently acquired in 1864 for approximately £1,200 and in May of the following year Hawksley - who had designed the works at Humbledon Hill, Fulwell and Cleadon - was asked to provide designs and specifications for the 'new works.'

The establishment of the pumping station was a major undertaking. Two wells needed to be sunk (sinking probably began in December 1865), six boilers and two large compound rotative beam engines had to be manufactured and assembled, the engine house, boiler house, smithy and chimney had to be built, two cooling ponds and a reservoir had to be dug, main delivery pipes laid, and dwellings for station personnel erected.

The first water was pumped in 1869, and evidently by early 1870 work had been completed to such an extent that the station was operating satisfactorily. It had cost £58,416, well over the estimated figure of £50,000, and the subsequent replacement of wooden temporary accommodation for the station personnel with permanent structures necessitated more expenditure.

For nearly the next century the station continued in operation, (normally its engines were run for alternate weeks), but a number of factors led the Sunderland and South Shields Water Company to decide to close the station as soon as an alternative supply - from the company's Derwent Reservoir - became available. Hence at 3pm on Saturday 1 July 1967 the commercial use of the station (the last steam powered station in the region) ceased when the steam valve was closed and the south engine slowed and stopped.

By this date interest in industrial archaeology was grow ing, and fortunately the company was sympathetic to the wishes of persons interested in the preservation of the pumping station. Among such was Stuart Smith, the assistant curator of Sunderland Museum. In 1968 he formed a group which began preservation work at Ryhope by covering the engines with grease to prevent corrosion and, in 1970, formed the Ryhope Engines Preservation Fund with the aim of maintaining the machinery in wor king order and transforming the station into a museum dealing with the history of water pumping and supply. Thankfully, this aim was attained and dedicated volunteers have maintained the site ever since.

65. The engine house under construction, with one of the beams being lifted into place

Description

Ryhope Pumping Station, which is flanked by cooling ponds to the north and south, could have been constructed with little or no embellishment, as was the case for instance with the works at Humbledon Hill. But this is not the case. In common with many other pumping stations, Ryhope is an attractive edifice with the large engine house, the principal part of the structure, enhanced by the provision of wall buttresses surmounted by finials, and by the spired ventilator crowning its roof.

The engine house is entered at its east end, through a doorway reached by stairs. Despite the size of the impressive machinery it contains, the atmosphere is not forbidding owing to the provision of substantial windows which bathe it in light.

Upon entering, one is soon flanked by the two engines, which are situated opposite each other on the north and south sides of the engine house. They are double-acting, compound, rotative beam engines which were made by R. & W. Hawthorn of Newcastle upon Tyne and cost £6,000. As noted, they are massive. Each of the beams, for instance, weighs 22 tons and had to be drawn to Ryhope by a team of forty horses. Furthermore, as Stafford Linsley has commented: 'It is not possible to see an entire engine from any single position as it occupies three and a half floors within the engine house.'

Three million gallons of water a day were pumped to the surface and discharged into a service reservoir (just to the east of the engine house), which was covered over in 1956. The water was brought to the surface in two stages via wells at the east and west ends of the engine house. From a depth of about 250ft the water was pumped up the main well, at the east end, to a height of 130ft below ground at which point it was discharged

66. Ryhope Pumping Station from the south

67. An early view of the interior of the engine house

through a 'staple' i.e., small tunnel, into the 'staple' well and then pumped to the surface. In all, the engines raised about a hundred million gallons of water during the century or so of their working life, a sufficient amount to make 3.2 trillion cups of tea.

The engine house is adjoined to the west by a block of four single storey gabled bays. Here, among other things, are the boilers. Originally there were six Cornish boilers but in 1908 they were replaced by three more advanced Lancashire boilers. The first boilers had occupied three of the bays, but their replacements are located in the two easternmost, while the third bay was transformed into a coal store. The westernmost bay always housed the smithy. Today, the westernmost bays partly house the museum devoted to the history of the site and the history of water pumping and supply in general. Finally, just to the west of this block is the chimney, which is nearly 160ft high and a prominent landmark.

Ryhope Pumping Station is one of the finest industrial monuments in the North East of England. It is an important reminder of the technological advancement which is a characteristic of the 19th century, and a credit to the dedicated individuals of the Ryhope Engines Trust who have ensured its survival. At several times a year, such as from Good Friday to Easter Monday and at weekends during the Christmas holiday, the engines are still run under steam for the benefit of visitors.

SOUTER LIGHTHOUSE

S outer Lighthouse lies on Lizard Point a short distance from South Shields and a couple of hundred yards or so from where limestone cliffs fall to the North Sea. On a fine day it has commanding views of much of the coastline of Northumberland and Yorkshire, while in normal conditions, Marsden Rock, a well-known limestone outcrop just off South Shields, is clearly visible.

Souter (pronounced Sooter), was built in 1871 to render shipping on the hazardous stretch of sea between the Tyne and Sunderland, at the mouth of the River Wear a few miles to the south, less hazardous.

It was not the first lighthouse in the area. In 1536 Henry VIII had granted a charter to the Guild of the Blessed Trinity at Newcastle which required it to 'found, build, make and frame of stone, lime and sand...two towers, one in the northern part of the Shelys [i.e. North Shields] at the entrance of the port of the said town, and the other upon a hill there fit and convenient for signals' etc. The towers were rebuilt in 1727, and replaced in 1808 by ones 60ft high. By this date Sunderland had also been furnished with a lighthouse. In 1801-2 its harbour engineer, Jonathan Pickernell, supervised the construction of a no longer extant octagonal lighthouse 76ft high on the north pier.

During the course of the 19th century the number of vessels plying the coast increased enormously. In large part this was due to the growth of industry. It was, for instance, cheaper to transport bulk cargoes such as coal and iron ore by sea than by rail. However, seaborne trade could prove dangerous and Whitburn Steel, a stretch of submerged rocks off Marsden and Whitburn, rendered travel along the coast between Sunderland and the Tyne more hazardous than would otherwise have been the case and contributed to the heavy losses experienced in these waters. In 1869 no less than 20 vessels came to grief between Sunderland and South Shields.

Demands for the provision of a further lighthouse for this section of coast thus grew. The responsibility for providing one now belonged to Trinity House, the national lighthouse authority for England and Wales, which was about to embark on a major light-house building programme with the result, states Patrick Beaver, that 'well before the end of the [19th] century the British coast was the best lighted of any.'

The man appointed to design Souter Lighthouse was James Douglass (1826-98), Chief Engineer to Trinity House, a man who had links with County Durham through his mother and had undergone part of his schooling at Newcastle upon Tyne. Douglass had many years' experience in the field of lighthouse construction. In 1847 he had become assistant to his father, who was Superintendent Engineer to Trinity House, and had helped him build Bishop Rock Lighthouse west of the Isles of Scilly. One of James Douglass' most daunting exploits, indeed perhaps the most daunting, was building Wolf Rock Lighthouse on a submerged reef eight miles south-west of Land's End. Construction work began in 1861 and was not completed until 1870, (by which date Douglass had been appointed Trinity House's Chief Engineer) and entailed Douglass and his men being tied to the rock to avoid being swept away by Atlantic rollers which battered the site. But he is best known for Eddystone Lighthouse, which was built in 1878-1882 (as a replacement for a previous lighthouse of the same name), which guides vessels into Plymouth harbour and upon its completion he received a knighthood.

In comparison with some of the projects Douglass had undertaken, building a land-based lighthouse such as Souter was a fairly straightforward task. Initially, he planned to build the station at Souter Point midway between the Tyne and the Wear. However, by 1870 he had decided to build at Lizard Point instead, about a mile to the north. The site had higher cliffs and was further from the worst of the industrial pollution emanating from Wearside, hence a light would be more visible from a shorter (and thus cheaper) tower. Because a Lizard Point lighthouse already existed in Cornwall the name 'Souter' was retained for the new lighthouse, which opened in January 1871.

When Souter opened Sir Frederick Arrow, the Deputy-Master of Trinity House, 'made bold to say that no lighthouse in any part of the world would bear comparison with it.' Souter was indeed advanced for it was the first lighthouse in the world built to be powered by Professor Holmes' alternating current magneto-electric generator, which was based on a principle discovered by Michael Faraday that a magnet could generate an electric current in a coil of wire which passed back and forth between its poles. An emergency oil lamp was however provided at Souter in case the electric light failed, but within the first eight years this only occurred on two occasions, one of them being due to the keeper on watch having fallen asleep.

The light was focused by a large rotating octagonal drum in the lantern. Each side of the drum consisted of seven vertical lenses which condensed and reflected the light and multiplied it 230 times, producing a beam of 700,000 candlepower. Not for nothing did Major Elliot, an American lighthouse expert who visited Souter soon after it began operating, comment: 'After leaving the Tyne at night we stood off from Souter Point to observe the light from the sea, and it certainly surpassed in brilliancy any I have ever seen, being so bright that at a distance of several miles well-defined shadows were cast upon...deck.'

68. Souter in the late 19th century. The boiler house chimney was removed in 1914 when the lighthouse was converted to oil. The foghorn house can be seen on the right.

Another novel feature of Souter was that Douglass had provided a turntable in the lantern which extended to the full diameter of the apparatus, something which not only made it steadier but also enabled the keepers to work on the inside of the apparatus while it was rotating.

By 1914 the machinery was past its prime and so changes were made which increased the light's range to over 20 miles. A larger lantern was built and a bigger lens installed on a wider turntable which, although weighing 4 tons in all, rotated easily for it rested on a bath of a ton of virtually frictionless mercury. Furthermore, in 1914 the light was changed from electricity to oil and this remained the case until 1952 when it reverted to electricity, using 4,500 watt bulbs capable of producing a beam equivalent to 1½ million candles.

At lighthouses prior to Souter half the light cast by the revolving beam was wasted by being projected inland. But at Souter Douglass devised a system so that this light could be used effectively. Via a series of prisms it was reflected down the tower and through a window 22ft below the lantern in an arc of 31 degrees over Sunderland Bay. Furthermore, to warn against heading towards especially dangerous rocks in the bay Douglass added another feature. As Major Elliot commented: 'The window through which this borrowed light passes is divided vertically into parts, the one on the western or land-side being red and the other white....When the fixed white light is seen, vessels will be in line of Mill Rock and Cape Carr Point, and when it changes to red, in that of Whitburn Sile [Steel], Hendon Rock, and White Stones.' After 1914 an oil-burning light and lenses were used instead of Douglass' series of prisms and this remained the case until the early 1950s when electric power was used again.

And what of Souter's foghorns? When visibility was reduced by inclement weather to less than two miles in daytime, or the lights of the Tyne and Wear piers could not be seen at night, the foghorns - located on a freestanding building to the east of the lighthouse tower - were operated, providing a four-second blast every forty-five seconds. Originally there was only one horn. It was painted white, looked much like a clay pipe, and faced directly out to sea. But by the early 20th century this had been replaced by two similarly shaped horns placed at such an angle that the sound would be projected up and down the coast. In time, these were replaced with the present trumpet-like horns, angled in the same manner, and even more powerful.

Souter remained in operation until 1988 when Trinity House decided to close the lighthouse owing to a decline in coastal shipping. It was thus sold to the National Trust in 1990, but continues to aid seafarers via an automatic radio beacon.

Description

A typical land-based lighthouse is painted white, with a black roof and green doors and windows sills, and Souter conforms to this pattern. Initially the lighthouse stood some 345 yards from the clifftop but erosion has brought the cliff edge significantly closer than was the case.

Moreover, originally Souter stood alone but this soon changed. In 1874 the Whitburn Coal Company began sinking Whitburn Colliery a short distance to the south of the lighthouse and thus a village - Marsden - rapidly began developing immediately to the north of Souter to accommodate employees and their families. The mine closed in 1968 and both the mine workings and the village have been demolished with the result that Souter is once again the dominant feature on this section of coastline.

The most eyecatching part of the lighthouse is of course the tower. It is over 75ft high and was built by a local man, Robert Allison of Whitburn, and consists of masonry covered in Portland cement to protect it from the weather. With the exception of the foghorn house, the rest of the station, comprising an engine and boiler house, coke store, workshop, storeroom and six cottages for the staff and their families, was built on the landward side of the tower around a square courtyard with a covered inner corridor. In each cottage a small entrance hall opened onto a central staircase hall which was flanked downstairs by the kitchen and parlour (which often doubled as the parents' bedroom) and by two bedrooms upstairs. If need be, spare bedrooms in the dwellings of unmarried keepers were borrowed by those with large families and doors connecting the adjoining cottages were used for this purpose. Each cottage had a front garden enclosed by a stone wall and a backyard with a wash-house, outside lavatory, and fuel store. Not surprisingly, life at a landbased lighthouse such as Souter was far less isolated and restricted than it was on a rock lighthouse. The census of 1881, for instance, records that Henry Millet, who had been in charge at Souter since it opened, had a household comprising his wife, eight children, an unmarried sister and a servant.

A substantial supply of water was required for the boilers which powered the light and foghorn, and as there were no springs or streams on the headland, Douglass installed 60,000 gallon capacity rainwater tanks into the foundations of the inner court-yard and outside the engine house.

Visitors to Souter first enter the shop, located in what was the boiler house and fuel store in the middle of the west range. From here one enters the adjoining engine room to the south. Originally this contained two of Professor Holmes' magneto-electric genera-

69. Souter Lighthouse from the south

70. Souter Lighthouse from the east

tors, as well as two Cornish boilers which consumed 100 tons of coke a year. Today, notable features of the engine room are two compressors which supplied compressed air to the foghorns. One of the compressors dates from 1961 and was electrically driven. If for some reason it failed, its diesel-powered companion would take over. The compressors pumped air into large circular storage tanks which stand near the north side of the room from where it was sent to the foghorns when required.

From the engine room visitors head into an adjoining room to the east where several items of interest are displayed and where a video recounts the history of the lighthouse. At the east end of this room is a corridor running north-south. A short walk to the north leads to one of the keeper's cottages which has been furnished as it would have appeared in the early days of the lighthouse. After examining this, one heads back along the corridor to another corridor which leads east to the tower. Here spiral stairs ascend to the lower lantern which has a window through which passed the middle light referred to above. Very steep stairs then lead to the upper lantern which also contains apparatus of interest. Owing to limitations of space, the number of people who can ascend the tower at any one time is regulated by staff, and anyone who suffers from vertigo would be wise to forgo this part of a tour of Souter. In addition to examining the apparatus in the upper lantern, on fine days one can enjoy extensive views of the coast for it is possible to see up to 80 miles in either direction.

As has been noted, Souter Lighthouse is owned by the National Trust. This is also true of much of the ground in its vicinity, which offers fine walks along the clifftops. Moreover, just to the north-west of the lighthouse one can see a battery of disused limekilns which are thought to date from the 1870s. They burnt limestone from an adjacent quarry, which had been worked since the early 19th century, and were fuelled by coal from Whitburn Colliery.

SOUTH SHIELDS ROMAN FORT

T he Roman fort at South Shields, (or *Arbeia* as it was evidently known towards the close of the Roman period), was an important one which defended a port at the mouth of the River Tyne and for many years served as a major supply base. It was situated in a commanding position on the south side of the river on a low headland formed by a bend in the Tyne, and had fine views of the river mouth and the sea.

The first excavation work at South Shields commenced in 1875 and continued into the following year. Between then and 1949-50 when Ian Richmond, one of the most talented archaeologists of his generation, conducted extensive excavations, no work was undertaken. Since then, however, several phases of excavation have occurred - the most recent commenced in 1983 and is still underway - and thus much of interest has been uncovered.

The fort was founded in the A.D. 160s but it is evident that there was an earlier Roman presence. Indeed, it has been suggested that an earth and timber fort was constructed at South Shields in the days of Agricola. Richmond, for example, commented: 'There is as yet no structural evidence for a first-century fort...though pottery suggests that one may have existed.' This was discounted by two archaeologists in 1979 who argued that the amount of early material was insufficient to support such a claim, but since 1983 the number of early finds has increased, making the idea of a late 1st century fort more plausible. The earliest structural remains at South Shields date from c.A.D. 125, and are thus contemporaneous with Hadrian's Wall. They appear to have belonged to a civil settlement (subsequently partly overlain by the fort founded in the 160s) which either developed outside the possible 1st century fort or one constructed in the days of Trajan or Hadrian and likely located just to the south or east of the excavated remains.

The present fort, a stone structure, was constructed in c.A.D. 163 and the builders were drawn from the Sixth Legion. It was built at a time when Hadrian's Wall was reoccupied after being temporarily abandoned in favour of the Antonine Wall (built between the Forth and the Clyde in the 140s). As first built, the fort comprised an area of 4.1 acres and its garrison appears to have consisted of 480 infantry and 120 cavalry. But it seems that by the close of the century the garrison's strength had been significantly reduced.

However, the fort was on the eve of a change which would increase its importance, for in c.A.D. 205-7 it was extended southward so that its size increased to 5.2 acres. Furthermore, it was divided in half by a substantial wall which was interrupted at its centre by the headquarters building or *principia*, which was substantially altered and provided with a new forecourt. Moreover, large-scale demolition of many of the fort's buildings was undertaken and thirteen stone granaries were erected instead in the northern half of the fort where the original double granary of the stone fort was also located. (Much of the fabric of the walls surrounding the original forecourt of the *principia* was incorporated in one of the granaries). In the southern half of the fort was the accommodation of the garrison, the Fifth Cohort of Gauls - which may have garrisoned the fort from the outset, c.A.D. 163, and certainly did so from this period until the late 3rd century - as well as two granaries which housed their provisions.

The fort was thus transformed into a substantial supply base and this was most probably part of the preparations made for the campaigns of the Emperor Septimus

Severus in Scotland in 208-10. The emperor may have intended conquering Scotland. If so, his death at York in 211 resulted in a new policy. Campaigning in Scotland ceased, and though part of the east coast appears to have been held for some years, henceforth Hadrian's Wall and its outpost forts marked the effective limit of Rome's hold on Britain.

In c.222-235 further changes occurred at South Shields. The dividing wall was removed and seven more granaries were evidently added to the supply base. One of these was constructed by converting the *principia* hall into a granary. Furthermore, the accommodation for the garrison was entirely rebuilt. So too was a new headquarters. Like the barracks, and six of the additional granaries, the new *principia* was situated in the southern half of the fort.

In all, it seems that there were twenty-four granaries and that they were arranged in three rows of eight across the width of the fort. Their storage capacity was considerable. Paul Bidwell, Principal Keeper of Archaeology for Tyne and Wear Museums, has recently commented, 'the original supply base could have held more than a month's supply of grain for what by the standards of the ancient world was an army of enormous size. Likewise, the enlarged supply base could have held something in the order of six months' supply for the entire garrison of Hadrian's Wall and the outpost forts.'

In the late 3rd or early 4th century much of the fort was destroyed by fire, the cause of which is unknown, and substantial demolition and rebuilding ensued. For one thing, a new headquarters building was constructed on the site of the original *principia* in the centre of the fort. Additionally, the eight southern granaries were converted into barracks and, in the south-west sector of the fort, two more barracks were erected. To their east a house was constructed which served as the residence of the commander.

This phase of rebuilding was probably associated with the arrival of a new garrison, a unit of Tigris Bargemen, which garrisoned the fort until the end of Roman rule in Britain in the early 5th century and with whose arrival the name *Arbeia* is linked. *Arbeia* is probably a Latin version of an Aramaic word meaning 'the place of the Arabs,' Aramaic being the language spoken in the area in which the bargemen were recruited.

Though some alterations were made during the final century or so of the fort's existence, (including the building of what appears to have been a church in the courtyard of the *principia*), no major rebuilding occurred. Indeed, there are possible signs of decline. In the courtyard house, for example, at least one of the dining rooms was abandoned and some of the heating systems went out of use.

Following the end of Roman rule in Britain the fort likely served as a stronghold for native rulers, and in time may have become the property of Anglian royalty before the site degenerated into farmland.

Description

As with other Roman forts, South Shields was rectangular in plan and was protected by parallel defensive ditches running round its circumference. Behind these was a strong wall with towers at each angle, while four strong gates gave access to the fort. The West Gate was reconstructed in the latter half of the 1980s and great care was taken to ensure as high a degree of accuracy as possible. It is by far the site's most striking feature. In fact, according to Bidwell: 'Nothing in Britain gives a better impression of the scale and magnificence of Roman military architecture.' It contains a number of rooms furnished with displays. One such is the quartermaster's store on the ground floor of the northernmost of the gate's two towers. Furthermore, it is worth ascending to the open platform above the gate's twin arches for this provides commanding views of the fort and its surroundings.

71. The reconstructed West Gate

The remains of one of the angle towers are located a short distance to the north of the West Gate, and not far to the east of this is the site of the North Gate.

Heading south from here, towards the headquarters in the centre of the fort, the visitor walks on grass which overlies several granaries, and beyond which can be seen the remains of the forecourt granary.

The plan of the original *principia* can be largely determined from the substantial remains, as can that of the headquarters built on the same site late in the 3rd or early 4th century. Both were built to a standard pattern: they had a colonnaded courtyard, a great hall, and rooms running along the rear of the hall. However, while the original *principia* faced north-west, the latter faced south-east: the original great hall, which as noted above had become a granary, was restored to its original function.

The strongroom of the rebuilt *principia* is a notable feature. It is a basement chamber solidly built in massive blocks, and housed valuables such as bullion in transit and the soldiers' savings. The stairs which gave access to it from the great hall to the south, survive. Moreover, a fragment of a window sill with sockets for iron bars can also be seen on its south side, indicating that it was lit from the hall. Above the strongroom was the shrine of the rebuilt *principia*. It was the most sacred part of the fort and was likewise entered from the hall via a flight of steps. Here a life-sized statue of the emperor was guarded night and day, and the standards of the unit garrisoning the fort were kept.

The strongroom was flanked by offices equipped with underfloor heating channels which are clearly visible. Furthermore, just outside the north-west corner of the strong-room is a well 23ft deep which functioned throughout the fort's history and originally lay in the courtyard of the first headquarters. As for the great hall itself, it occupied the full width of the *principia* and contained a platform from which the commandant could address soldiers and dispense justice. The remains of two tribunals can be seen. Such a platform was always located on the right-hand side of a great hall. Hence when the *principia* was rebuilt facing in the opposite direction to its predecessor, the reconstituted great hall was provided with a platform on its right-hand side.

Running along the south side of the great hall are the foundations of five rooms which belonged to the original headquarters building. In contrast, the columns here are relics of the courtyard of the rebuilt *principia*.

To the west of the head-quarters building, and near the west gate, are the remains of a double granary, one of the original buildings of the fort. It was demolished in the

72. The strongroom, with the West Gate in the background

late 3rd or early 4th century. To the south lie later granaries which, as noted above, were converted into barracks during the phase of rebuilding associated with the destruction of the double granary.

The southern part of the fort also contains the remains of the headquarters building constructed c.222-235 (a strongroom, two offices and part of the great hall are visible), and those of the courtyard house built to the south-east in the late 3rd or early 4th century. The latter measured 138ft by 79ft and was ranged around a central courtyard. The complete plan has been uncovered, including formal dining rooms for use in

73. A general view across the fort, with the remains of the principia in the foreground

summer and winter, and a set of baths, and the house is said to be 'the best understood commanding officer's house in any fort in the Roman Empire.'

A short distance to the north of the courtyard house, and in the fort's east wall, one can see the south-east corner of the original fort. Upon following the newer walling (which dates from when the fort was extended southward to form the supply base), the remains of a latrine are soon visible, roughly halfway between the original south-east corner and that of the enlarged fort. Finally, as far as the fort is concerned, it is worth noting what survives of the tower in the south-west angle. Its walls stand to a height of six courses and consist of well-cut masonry.

Excavations have indicated that in Roman times a parade ground was situated outside the north-east angle of the fort, while it appears that the civil settlement occupied much of the area to the west of the fort. The cemetery which served both the settlement and garrison, evidently lay south-west of the fort along a road which connected South Shields with a north-south road, known today as Cade's Road, in the vicinity of Wrekenton.

The cemetery has yielded two famous 2nd century tombstones: one of a woman called Regina, the other, of Victor the Moor. Regina was a Catuvellaunian, and thus from south-east England. The tombstone was erected by her husband, Barates, a trader who hailed from the city of Palmyra in modern Syria. Prior to becoming his wife, Regina had been his slave. Victor was likewise a freed slave, in this case, that of a soldier who evidently served at South Shields. Both tombstones are on display in the site's museum, which opened in 1953.

South Shields Roman Fort is administered by Tyne and Wear Museums, and access is free. It is interesting to note that since the reconstruction of the West Gate the number of visitors has increased dramatically. In 1983, for instance, prior to the gate's reconstruction, there were less than 6,000, but in 1995 some 74,383 people visited the fort which has become one of the most popular archaeological sites in the north of England.

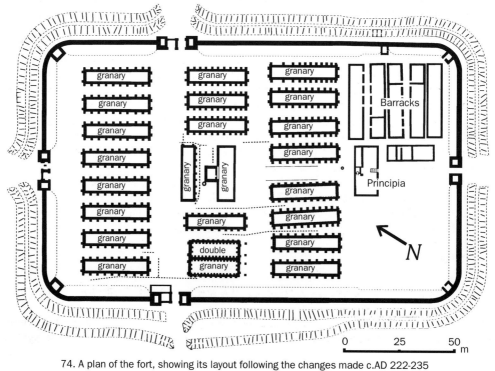

74. A plan of the fort, showing its layout following the changes made c.AD 222-235

TEES COTTAGE PUMPING STATION

Two miles west of the centre of Darlington in southern Durham stands the former Darlington Waterworks - now known as Tees Cottage Pumping Station - founded in 1849 to improve Darlington's water supply.

The waterworks was not established to supply a new community, for Darlington was a historic town dating from Saxon times which had been granted borough status in the 12th century and had been described by John Leland in the Tudor era as 'the best market town in the bishopric, saving Durham.' By the mid 18th century it had become famous as a centre of linen manufacture, and as the century drew to a close it briefly had a greater concentration of mills than any other town in England.

During the early decades of the 19th century Darlington's traditional industrial base came under pressure from elsewhere and so the town's entrepreneurs, headed by a member of the Pease family, realized the necessity of diversifying. Central to their plans was the establishment of a rail link with Stockton-on-Tees which would give them access to the sea, enabling them to benefit from County Durham's expanding coal trade. As a result, the Stockton and Darlington Railway opened in 1825 and, in addition to carrying passengers, transported coal from mines well inland via Darlington to docks at Stockton. Within less than a decade more than 30 collieries were using the line and Darlington had begun to boom, not only benefiting from a significant drop in the price of coal, but also from the establishment of a new industry, locomotive engineering. In 1851 its population had climbed to 11,600 people.

By this date the Darlington Gas and Water Company had been recently established. It was founded shortly after a sanitary committee under the chairmanship of John Pease had undertaken a survey of Darlington's water supply which revealed that 921 dwellings relied on 393 private pumps, 1,470 dwellings used 19 public pumps, and 8 dwellings, draw wells. One of the company's objectives was to improve the town's water supply by drawing water from the Tees and so in 1849 substantial waterworks were opened beside the river and proceeded to deliver water to Darlington through a system of pipes and reservoirs. The water had a peaty colour and was thus criticised. But it was much softer than the water the inhabitants were used to, and as William Fordyce recorded in the 1850s, one of the town's brewers declared that from 8 bushels of malt he could produce 18 gallons of ale more using Tees water than by what he had obtained from a pump, and that the ale was of a superior quality than had been the case.

In 1854 Darlington Local Board of Health took over the works which remained in the hands of Darlington Corporation until 1974 when the site passed to Northumbrian Water. It remained in commercial use until 1980 when it passed into the hands of a voluntary body, the Tees Cottage Pumping Station Preservation Trust.

Description

Tees Cottage Pumping Station is located on the south side of Coniscliffe Road and is bounded to the south by the Tees.

The site is entered via an entrance hall at the east end. This is adjoined by a room known as the Gas Producer Plant, where gas was produced by burning anthracite. The

75. Tees Cottage's Beam Engine House

equipment is no longer in working order. The gas was used to power a 220 b.h.p. gas engine dating from 1913 (located immediately to the west) with a pumping capacity capable of delivering 1,800 gallons per minute to the town and 2,000 g.p.m. from the river to filters for treatment. The engine became operational again in 1985 after years of disuse and is now operated using the town gas supply.

From the Gas Engine House one heads west towards the Beam Engine House, and en route passes two former filter beds which are now used as reservoirs: a third is located to the south of the Gas Engine House.

Before entering the Beam Engine House, a three-storey structure dating from the early 20th century, it is advisable to visit the Boiler House located in an original range of buildings adjoining to the west. This contains Lancashire boilers dating from 1902. Both are 28ft long by 7ft 6in. and have a working pressure of up to 100 p.s.i. Steam generated by them is piped to the Beam Engine House, which is entered from the north via a flight of steps. Its two cylinder steam compound rotative beam engine dates from 1904 and has a pumping capacity capable of raising 1,900 g.p.m. from the Tees for treatment and delivering 1,700 g.p.m. to Darlington.

The west side of the Beam Engine House is adjoined by a building which housed the original beam engine and which is now used as a workshop, while this is in turn adjoined by the Electric Pump House, (against the north side of the Boiler House), where two electric pumps were installed in 1926 with a combined pumping capacity exceeding that of both the gas and beam engines which were thus reduced to standbys. Moreover, pumping capacity was subsequently increased. Unlike the gas and steam engines, however, the pumps are no longer operated.

76. The Boiler House, showing a boiler and members
of the Tees Cottage Preservation Trust

In the far corner of the site, to the south of the Gas Engine House and close to the river, stands the Blacksmith's Shop. Here blacksmiths can sometimes be seen at work, using the oldest working equipment at Tees Cottage.

Finally, a miniature railway runs around much of the site. It is the responsibility of a group known as Cleveland Model Engineers, and transports visitors who wish to use it back and forth.

WASHINGTON OLD HALL

Washington Old Hall lies in pleasant grounds overlooked by the church of St Mary the Virgin on a wooded hill just to the north. It is situated in an old village which since the 1960s has been enveloped by Washington New Town.

The hall mostly dates from the 17th century. However, part of the building dates from the medieval period when the early ancestors and relations of America's first president, George Washington, held the vill from the Bishop of Durham.

The progenitor of the Washington family was William de Hertburn, a well-born individual who exchanged Hertburn near Stockton on Tees for Washington with Bishop Hugh du Puiset shortly before 1180. William assumed the name Washington, (or Wessington as it then was) for the manor house here was his principal residence.

Members of the family continued living at Washington for several generations and were persons of some consequence. It is significant that Edward I visited Washington in September 1304 while heading south from the Scottish border. The Washingtons would have spent much of their time in administrative work or in attending the Bishops of Durham. Moreover, some also participated in military ventures. One is recorded as having fought at the Battle of Lewes in 1264; another distinguished himself at Neville's Cross in 1346, while his son and successor Sir William, was captured at Otterburn in 1388.

Sir William died in 1399 without male issue. His only child, Eleanor, soon married Sir William Tempest of Studley Royal, Yorkshire, and Washington passed into his hands. The couple had a daughter, Dionisia, who married Sir William Mallory and descendants of the match continued in possession of Washington until 1613 when the manor was sold to the Bishop of Durham, William James, for £4,000.

The wealthy prelate, who was thrice married, died in 1617, leaving Washington (and land at Hetton-le-Hole) to his son, Francis, who was then sixteen. Francis married a merchant's daughter in 1623 and spent his life as a country gentleman, preferring to live at Hetton-le-Hole than at Washington, which stayed in the possession of the James family until the death of his grandson, William James of Washington in 1663, whereupon it was left to William's sisters and their spouses.

Following the division of the manor the hall suffered neglect and was subsequently converted into tenements. By 1936 it had fallen into such a state that it was condemned as unfit for habitation. It was saved from demolition by a local preservation committee, and restoration ensued. Work was interrupted by the war, but in 1955 the hall was officially opened by the American ambassador, Mr Charles Sumner Bird.

Description

Washington Old Hall is approached from the west. Essentially, it is a typical early 17th century manor house, and is usually said to have been built by Bishop James, but Pevsner states that it was built about 1623, some years after the prelate's death. It comprises a two-storey central block, flanked to the east and west by projecting three-storey gabled wings, while projecting from the centre of the south front is another wing of three storeys through which the hall is entered: formerly the manor house was entered from the north and the outline of a central porch can still be seen.

77. Washington Old Hall from the south

The Great Hall - built upon the foundations of its medieval predecessor - is centrally placed on the ground floor and is directly north of the entrance lobby. It has a finely beamed ceiling, mullioned windows and, at the east end, a fireplace which was brought to Washington from Newburn Manor on the Tyne. (In medieval times the dais and high table would have been situated at this end of the hall).

From the east end of the Great Hall one has access to the two rooms on the ground floor of the adjoining wing. The beautifully grained oak panelling here was brought to Washington from an old manor house at Abbots Langley and was given by Miss Mabel Choate in memory of her father, a former American Ambassador to Britain.

The wall separating the Great Hall from the kitchen to the west is unplastered and has two arched doorways dating from the days of the medieval manor house. The kitchen is a fine room, largely of medieval date, and occupies the ground floor of the west wing. It has two mullioned windows of four-lights (one in the north wall, the other in the south) and a smaller window in the west wall near the 17th century fireplace with its wide, low arch and open hearth. Like all the principal rooms, the kitchen has a finely beamed ceiling and interesting furniture.

The upper floors are reached via a staircase in the entrance wing. (The stairs were brought to Washington from the White Hart Hotel, Guildford, during the period of restoration). Rooms on the upper floors are used as a community centre. Here too, is the Bedroom, with its fine oak bed dating from the 17th century, and its original Tudor-style fireplace.

WITTON CASTLE

W itton is a picturesque castle situated in pleasant grounds on the south side of the River Wear, and about half a mile from the village of Witton-le-Wear.

The castle is perhaps best known as the former residence of the Eure family, which traced its descent from Hugh, the second son of one of King John's baronial opponents, John FitzRobert, the lord of Warkworth in Northumberland. Hugh adopted the name Eure from a manor in Buckinghamshire of which he was lord, and it was retained by subsequent heads of the family.

Just when the Eures gained possession of the manor of Witton is uncertain. We do know, however, that in 1322 Sir John de Eure (who had been captured at Bannockburn in 1314), was killed nearby at Bishop Auckland in the erroneous belief that he was one of the enemies of Edward II. We first hear that the Eures were in possession of Witton during the episcopate of Richard Bury (1333-45), for he pardoned Ralph, the brother and heir of Sir Robert de Eure - who held Witton - for marrying without licence.

On 23 September 1410 the then head of the family, Sir Ralph, was granted permission by Bishop Langley to 'inclose his manor...with a wall of lime and stone...and build a fortress thereon...' Construction work had, however, already begun. Sir Nikolaus Pevsner suggests that it may have done so in about 1370, while Malcolm Hislop believes that at least some of the fabric probably dates from the 1390s.

The fact that work on Witton Castle commenced before the requisite licence was obtained from the Bishop of Durham moved the Victorian historian, William Fordyce, to state that 'none but such as supposed themselves to be almost above the law' would have acted in such a manner'. Sir Ralph Eure was indeed a man of consequence, for in addition to his lands in Durham he possessed estates in Northumberland and Yorkshire and, as R.L. Storey has commented, 'was one of the wealthiest landowners in northern England below the ranks of the peerage.' Furthermore, he was high in royal favour and as Langley's steward was the most important member of the prelate's lay administration, for the holder of this office (until the mid 15th century) had authority amounting to a general superintendence of the government of the palatinate of Durham.

In 1422 Eure was succeeded by his eldest son, Sir William. The latter, who had spent part of his youth in Langley's household, became involved in a bitter dispute with the bishop in 1432. He was summoned to Langley's chancery and asked to give a reason why lands in his possession should not be seized by the bishop. Owing to an error on the part of the chancery, Eure had been able to enter into possession of the property in question at the time he had received livery of his father's estates (14 September 1422), even though the lands had been acquired without licence from Langley. The fact that Sir William was many months in arrears with rent he owed for mines he had leased from the bishop added fuel to the fire.

A protracted dispute resulted, and in 1433 Eure was among discontented tenants of the bishop who instigated a major constitutional assault on the palatine status of the bishopric of Durham. This measure failed, however, and Langley's suit against Eure continued. Judgement was given in the bishop's favour in Durham's chancery in August 1435: a decision which was upheld by the court of King's Bench following an appeal by Eure.

This audacious figure was succeeded by his son Ralph, who was 'slayne on palmeson-daye' 1461 at the Battle of Towton during the Wars of the Roses. His great-grandson, William, served as Sheriff of Durham from 1519 until 1523 and as Sheriff of Northumberland in 1526-7. Furthermore he was appointed Warden of the East March before 1538 and as such was responsible for the maintenance of law and order in the far north-east of England. He was created Baron Eure in 1544 and died four years later. His eldest son, 'one of the bravest men of a military race,' had been killed fighting against the Scots and so the title passed to his grandson.

The fourth Lord Eure sold Witton to Sir William Forster in the 1620s, preferring to reside at Malton Castle, Yorkshire. Witton soon passed into other hands, and has been owned by several families and individuals over the years. In the mid 19th century it was purchased by the extremely wealthy Lambton family, whose principal residence was Lambton Castle, a mock-Gothic structure of recent date near Chester-le-Street. Interestingly, at one time Sir Thomas Lawrence's famous portrait of young Master Lambton - the Red Boy - was hung at Witton. The youngster immortalized by Lawrence was the son of the most famous Lambton of them all, 'Radical Jack' (1792-1840), who was created Earl of Durham in 1833 and in whose honour Penshaw Monument was erected near Sunderland.

Witton is still owned by the Lambtons and has been developed as a caravan site.

Description

As completed in the early 15th century, the castle comprised an oblong keep situated in the north-east corner of a courtyard which also housed ancillary buildings. Over the centuries, however, other buildings have been added to the castle owing to changing tastes and requirements but fortunately much of medieval interest has survived.

The curtain wall is 5ft thick and has gateways in the middle of its east and west sides, and over each entrance is a machicolated gallery supported by double corbels. The ground falls away steeply about 92ft east of the east gateway to form a gully, thereby once providing a natural obstacle to anyone who wished to storm the castle.

It is interesting to note that there were rows of holes high up in the exterior masonry of the curtain wall. These were intended to receive the supports of projecting parapeted wooden platforms from which the wall itself could be better defended. The parapet of the curtain wall is embattled and the crenels were provided with pivoted iron shutters, each of which could be pivoted by means of a socket at one side of the embrasure and a slot in the stonework at the other end. Thus, in times of emergency, these could be raised to allow members of the garrison on the broad sentry walk to fire, and then be lowered again to provide protection.

Each corner of the curtain wall was provided with a bartizan. Three remain. That at the north-east angle is the least

78. Witton Castle from the south-east

79. The castle as seen from the courtyard. The keep is on the right

interesting and merits little attention, but the south-east bartizan projects more boldly from the wall and contains a chamber. The room is circular and has three loopholes in its outer wall. The roof of the bartizan has a crenellated parapet and can be reached by means of a stairway corbelled out from the inner face of the parapet of the curtain wall.

The south-west bartizan is almost square in plan, unlike the others which are round, and its weight is partly supported by a squinch across the angle of the curtain wall. Like the bartizan just described, its has a guard-chamber. This has a fireplace with an octagonal chimney shaft. Moreover, the room has two doorways which enable it to be entered from the south and west sections of the curtain wall. The roof of the bartizan has an embattled parapet and can be reached via a stairway corbelled out from the inner face of the parapet of the west side of the curtain wall.

Formerly, there was a bartizan at the north-west corner of the curtain wall. It was destroyed in the late 18th century when the present buildings adjoining the west side of the keep were built to provide additional living accommodation.

The courtyard itself is almost square. It measures 156ft from east to west by 152ft, and was used during the Border Wars as a place of refuge by tenants of the manor. On the south side of the courtyard, and centrally placed, is a substantial tower-like building probably constructed during the 16th century.

The keep measures 54ft from east to west by 29ft, and on its north side projects just beyond the curtain wall. It has a turret at each corner, rising above the roof. Those on the east side project diagonally like buttresses and have crenellated parapets which are flush with the fronts of the turrets but machicolated on either side, an unusual feature found elsewhere in the county at Raby and Brancepeth. The west turrets are larger - this is especially true of the south-west turret - and again have embattled parapets though they are devoid of machicolation. On the battlements of the south-west turret are two carved figures similar to those which can seen elsewhere, at for example Hylton and Raby. The keep has a barrel-vaulted basement. A newel stair ascends from the basement to what was the Great Hall at first floor level. None of the windows at this level, or elsewhere in the keep for that matter, is original.

The long range extending west from the west end of the keep dates from the late 18th and 19th centuries and was built to provide more living space. As with the keep, rooms here are now used for refreshments etc by visitors to Witton.

GLOSSARY

AISLE: passage alongside a nave, transept etc. of a church or the main body of some other building, separated from it by columns etc.

ANNULET: a motif of the 12th and 13th centuries consisting of a ring round a shaft.

APSE: in churches, a semicircular or polygonal end to a chancel, aisle, etc.

ARCADE: a series of arches supported by piers. *Blind* or *blank arcade* - series of arches supported by piers attached to the surface of a wall.

ASHLAR: squared blocks of masonry laid in regular courses.

ATTACHED: see 'Engaged Column'

BAILEY: defended enclosure or courtyard of a castle.

BARBICAN: outer fortification defending a gateway.

BAROQUE: an exuberant style of architecture of the 17th and part of the 18th centuries, characterized by curving forms, extravagant decoration and spatially complex compositions. The style was first used in this country in the latter half of the 17th century. Vanbrugh's Seaton Delaval Hall (Northumberland) and Castle Howard (North Yorkshire) are famous examples of English Baroque.

BARREL-VAULT: see 'Vault'

BARTIZAN: a square or round corbelled turret frequently at the corner of a tower etc.

BATTLEMENT: a parapet with indentations (embrasures or crenels), alternating with solid portions (merlons).

BAYS: divisions of a building defined by regular vertical features such as buttresses.

BILLET: Romanesque ornament consisting of several bands of small half-cylindrical or rectangular blocks placed at regular intervals.

BOSS: an enriched ornamental block usually covering the intersections of ribs in a vault.

BUTTRESS: projecting mass of masonry or brickwork supporting a wall, or resisting the lateral thrust of a vault etc. *Angle buttresses* - two meeting at an angle of 90 degrees at the corner of a building. *Diagonal buttress* - one placed against the right angle formed by two walls and more or less equiangular with both. *Flying buttress* - an arch or half-arch transmitting the thrust of a vault or roof from the upper part of a wall to a free-standing support.

CANOPY: a projection or hood over a door, window, etc or the covering of a tomb.

CAPITAL: head of a column etc; it is normally decorated.

CHANCEL: the part of the east end of a church in which the principal altar is located. Also often applied to the entire east limb of a church.

CHAPTER HOUSE: room where monks met daily to hear a chapter of the monastic Rule and to discuss business.

CHEVRON: zigzag Norman ornament of the 12th century.

CHOIR: the part of a church where services are sung. Also often applied to the east limb of a cruciform church.

CLASSICAL: term applied to Greek and Roman architecture and styles inspired by it.

CLAUSTRAL: pertaining to the cloister.

CLERESTORY: the upper stage of a church elevation and pierced by windows.

CLOISTER: in a monastic establishment, a covered walkway around an open quadrangle (garth).

COFFERED: a ceiling decorated with sunken square or polygonal ornamental panels.

COLONNETTE: a small column or shaft.

COLUMN: a vertical structural member typically consisting of a shaft with a base and a capital.

COMPOUND PIER: a pier consisting of a solid core surrounded by attached or detached shafts, or consisting of a bundle of shafts.

CORBEL: a projecting stone or piece of timber to support a weight.

COURSE: continuous layer of bricks etc. in a wall.

COVED CEILING: one which has a pronounced concave curve joining the walls to a flat central area.

CRENELLATED: a battlemented wall.

CROSSING: in a church, the space at the junction of the nave, transepts and chancel.

CUPOLA: term usually applied to a small dome on a circular or polygonal base crowning a turret etc.

CURTAIN WALL: the outer wall of a castle and often punctuated by towers.

DAIS: raised platform at the end of a room.

DECORATED: historical division of English Gothic architecture c.1290 to c.1340. A sumptuous style characterized by rich decoration of surfaces, flowing and reticulated tracery, the ogee arch, and lofty spires. The style is not well represented in County Durham.

DEMI-COLUMN: a column which is half-sunk into a wall.

DOGTOOTH: typical Early English decoration consisting of a series of pyramidal flowers of four petals.

EARLY ENGLISH: term applied to the style of English Gothic architecture of c.1190 to c.1290. An essentially refined style, chiefly characterized by lancet windows, which are often grouped together. Other motifs include columns surrounded by marble shafts and dogtooth and stiff-leaf ornament. It is well represented in County Durham.

EMBATTLED: furnished with battlements.

ENGAGED COLUMN: a column partly merged into a wall or pier.

ENTABLATURE: in Classical architecture, the horizontal members above a column.

FERETORY: the place behind the high altar containing the principal shrine of a church.

FINIAL: decorative feature at the top of a buttress etc.

FLUTING: series of concave grooves.

FOIL: Leaf-like ornamentation in windows etc. Trefoil, quatrefoil, cinquefoil etc. express the number of lobes in a shape.

FOLIATED: ornamented with representations of foliage.

GABLE: area of wall - often triangular - at the end of a double pitched roof.

GALLERY: in a church, the intermediate storey above the aisle and below the clerestory, and looking through arches to the nave etc.

GARDEROBE: individual lavatory in a medieval building.

GOTHIC: a general term used for the architecture of western Europe c.1140 to c.1530. The style appeared in England in the third quarter of the 12th century at places such as Canterbury and was introduced to Durham in c.1192 by Bishop Hugh du Puiset. Gothic buildings have less massively built walls, larger windows and more lofty proportions than the earlier Romanesque style and characteristic features are rib-vaults, pointed arches, flying buttresses, window tracery and spires. English Gothic architecture is usually divided into three phases: Early English, Decorated and Perpendicular. There was a revival of Gothic motifs in Durham during the 17th century and a general revival commenced in England in the mid 18th century. A famous example of Gothic architecture is Salisbury Cathedral in Wiltshire, which is essentially Early English.

GUILLOCHE: an ornamental band with paired ribbons flowing in interlaced curves.

HEADSTOP: see 'Stops.'

HERRINGBONE WORK: masonry or brickwork in zigzag courses.

HOODMOULD: projecting moulding over an arch or lintel to throw off water.

IMPOST: a member in a wall upon which the end of an arch rests.

JAMB: one of the straight sides of a doorway, window, etc.

KEEL-MOULDING: moulding shaped like the keel of a ship.

KEEP: the main tower of a castle.

LANCET WINDOW: slender window with a pointed arch.

LANTERN: 1). in Gothic architecture the term usually applies to a tower open from below and commonly found over the crossing of a church. 2). a chamber at the top of a lighthouse enclosing the light.

LIERNE: minor rib connecting bosses or intersections of principal ribs in Gothic vaulting.

LIGHT: architectural term for a compartment of a window.

LOOPHOLE: a small or narrow opening in a wall through which arrows etc. could be fired.

LOUVRE: opening in the roof of a room to let smoke escape.

MACHICOLATIONS: openings between the corbels of a projecting parapet through which boiling water etc. could be dropped on assailants.

MOTTE-AND-BAILEY: a castle comprising an earth mound (motte) surmounted by a tower, and an attached enclosure (bailey) at a lower level, and defended by a ditch and palisade.

MOULDING: a decorative band or edge.

MULLION: a vertical bar dividing a window into lights.

NAVE: the main part of a church and where the congregation assembles: often flanked by aisles.

NEWEL STAIR: one ascending round a central supporting post (newel).

NOOK-SHAFT: a shaft set in the angle of a wall or the angle of the jamb of a door etc.

NORMAN: see Romanesque.

OGEE ARCH: a pointed arch, each side of which has a double curve, the lower concave, the upper convex.

ORATORY: small chapel in a church or house for private devotions.

ORDER: one of a series of concentric stages - shafts for instance - receding towards the opening of a doorway etc.

ORIEL WINDOW: one which projects from the face of a building and is always on an upper floor.

PALLADIAN: a style of architecture based on the work of the Italian architect, Andrea Palladio, (1508-80), and introduced into England in the first quarter of the 17th century though the style only started becoming fashionable in c.1715. It is far less exuberant than Baroque and is characterized by good taste, harmonious proportions, and self-restraint.

PARAPET: a low wall for protection at any sudden drop.

PEDIMENT: in Classical architecture, a formalized gable over a portico etc.

PERPENDICULAR: the final phase of English Gothic architecture c.1340 to c.1530, and a marked contrast to the richness and great variety of the preceding Decorated phase. It is characterized by emphasis on straight verticals and horizontals. Among other character-istics are subdued window tracery and a fondness for lofty towers such as the crossing tower of Durham Cathedral. King's College Chapel, Cambridge, is a famous example of the style, which is not well represented in County Durham.

PIER: a strong vertical support for arches etc.

PILASTER: shallow pier attached to a wall.

PINNACLE: a relatively small vertical structure capping a buttress etc.

PORTICO: a porch which is open on at least one side, and is enclosed by columns which support the roof and often a pediment.

PORTICUS: room of variable size and function attached to a church: often a side-chapel.

PRESBYTERY: the eastern part of a church containing the main altar.

QUOINS: stones at the angles of a building. *Side-alternate quoining* consists of stones laid on their sides with their longer faces alternately along the respective walls. The term 'megalithic' is often used when the stones are of a large size.

REREDORTER: a building containing monastic latrines.

REREDOS: ornamental screen behind an altar

RESPOND: a half-pier bonded into a wall and supporting one end of an arch.

ROCOCO: the last phase of the Baroque style. It originated in France c.1720 and was current in Britain and on the continent until c.1760. It is characterized by its elegant refinement of plasterwork etc.

ROMANESQUE: a term applied to the style of architecture which is often called Norman in England, and was current in the 11th and 12th centuries. It is characterized by massively built walls, round arches, small windows, zigzag ornament, very robust columns, and clearly defined spatial units.

ROSE WINDOW: circular window with patterned tracery around the centre.

RUBBLE: masonry comprised of stones either partly or entirely in a rough state.

RUSTICATION: masonry consisting of blocks with recessed joints and, in many cases, an artificially roughened surface. It is intended to give the impression of strength.

SHAFT: a slender column.

SPANDREL: triangular space between two arches or between an arch and its containing rectangle.

SPLAY: a sloping chamfered surface cut into a wall. A splayed loophole, for instance, is much wider internally than externally.

SQUINCH: arch across the angle between two walls to support a superstructure.

STIFF-LEAF: Early English foliage ornamentation consisting of many lobed shapes.

STOPS: ornamental projecting stones at the ends of hoodmoulds etc. carved in various forms such as human heads or bunches of flowers.

STRING-COURSE: a horizontal band of masonry along the face of a wall from which it usually projects.

THROUGH-STONES: stones which extend the full thickness of a wall.

TRACERY: ornamental work in the head of a window (and elsewhere such as on blank arcading) and usually formed by the curving and interlacing of bars of stone. *Geometrical tracery* was in vogue in the latter half of the 13th century and the early years of the 14th, and consists of circles or foils within circles. *Reticulated tracery* is typical of the early decades of the 14th century and consists entirely of circles drawn into ogee shapes at top and bottom to create a net-like appearance.

TRANSEPTS: the transverse portions of a cross-shaped church.

TRANSITIONAL: the term applied to the architecture of c.1175-c.1190 during the transition from Romanesque to Early English.

TRANSOM: a horizontal bar across the lights of a window.

TRANSVERSE ARCH: in vaulting, an arch which divides one compartment of vaulting from another.

TUNNEL-VAULT: see 'Vault.'

TURRET: a small tower, usually attached to a building.

UNDERCROFT: a vaulted room - sometimes below ground - beneath the principal upper room.

VAULT: an arched stone ceiling, sometimes imitated in wood or plaster. *Barrel-* or *Tunnel-Vault* - one which looks like a continuous circular arch: the most basic vault. *Groin-vault* - one composed of two tunnel-vaults intersecting at right-angles. *Rib-vault*: a more attractive vault consisting of arched ribs and cells or compartments of masonry between the ribs. Rib-vaults can be very ornate, depending on the number of ribs employed.

VAULTING-SHAFT: a shaft supporting a transverse arch etc. of a vault.

VENETIAN WINDOW: a window with three openings, of which the central one is arched and wider than the others.

VOUSSOIRS: wedge-shaped stones forming an arch.

WATERLEAF: a broad, leaf-shaped motif with a tied-ribbon effect at the top. Often used to ornament capitals in the latter half of the 12th century.

BIBLIOGRAPHY

Abbreviations

AA 1,2,3, etc., Archaeologia Aeliana, series 1,2,3, etc.
AND - Anglo-Norman Durham 1093-1193, eds. D. Rollason, M. Harvey, M. Prestwich, 1993.
AS - Antiquities of Sunderland.
DAJ - Durham Archaeological Journal
DNB - Dictionary of National Biography
EHR - English Historical Review
NH - Northern History
TAASDN - Transactions of the Architectural and Archaeological
    Society of Durham and Northumberland
VCH - Victoria County History (Durham)

Alcock, L., *Quantity or Quality: Anglian graves in* Bernicia, 'Angles, Saxons and Jutes: Essays presented to J.N.L. Myres', ed. V.I. Evison, 1982.
Atkinson, F., *Industrial Archaeology: top ten sites in North East England*, 1971.
Austin, D., *Barnard Castle*, 1988.
Battiscombe, C.F., *Introduction*, in 'The Relics of St Cuthbert' ed C.F. Battiscombe, 1956.
Bayley, K., *Political History*, VCH vol.II, ed. W. Page, 1907.
Beaver, P., *A History of Lighthouses*, 1971.
Beddow, N., *Interpreting the Saxon Sundial at Escomb*, DAJ., vol.7., 1991.
Bonner, G., *Bede and Medieval Civilization*, Anglo-Saxon England, 2, 1973.
Boyle, J.R., *The County of Durham*, 1892.
Bradshaw, F., *Social and Economic History*, VCH vol.II ed. W. Page, 1907.
Bradshaw, F., *The Black Death in the Palatinate of Durham*, AA 3, vol.III, 1907.
Butler, L., & Given-Wilson, C., *Medieval Monasteries of* Great Britain, 1979.
Chadwick, L., *Lighthouses and Lightships*, 1971.
Cambridge, E., *Early Romanesque Architecture in North-East England: A Style and its Patrons*, AND, 1993.
Carver, M.O.H., *Early Medieval Durham: the archaeological* evidence, 'Medieval Art and Architecture at Durham Cathedral', 1980.
Cherry, B., *Ecclesiastical Architecture*, 'The Archaeology of Anglo-Saxon England' ed. D.M. Wilson, 1976.
Clack, P., *The Book of Durham City*, 1985.
Cornford, M.E., *Religious Houses*, VCH vol.II ed. W. Page, 1907.
Cramp, R.J., *Excavations at the Saxon Monastic Sites of Wearmouth and Jarrow: an Interim Report*, 'Medieval Archaeology,' 13, 1969
Cramp, R.J., *The Anglo-Saxons and Rome*, TAASDN, new series vol.III, 1974.
Cramp, R.J., *Monastic Sites*, 'The Archaeology of Anglo-Saxon England' ed. D.M. Wilson, 1976.
Creighton, M., *Antony Bek*, DNB vol. IV, 1885.
Curry, I., *Aspects of the Anglo-Norman design of Durham Cathedral*, AA 5, vol.XIV, 1986.
Dobson, B., *Roman Durham*, TAASDN, new series vol.II, 1970. Dobson, R.B., *Durham Priory, 1400-1450*, 1973.
Draper, P., *The Nine Altars at Durham and Fountains*, 'Medieval Art and Architecture at Durham Cathedral', 1980.
Drury, J.L., *Durham Palatinate Forest Law and Administration, specially in Weardale up to 1440*, AA 5, vol.VI, 1978.
Fell, C.I., and Hildyard, E.J.W., *Prehistoric Weardale - a new survey*, AA 4, vol. XXXI, 1953.
Fenton-Thomas, C., *Pollen Analysis as an Aid to the Reconstruction of Patterns of Land-Use and Settlement in the Tyne-Tees Region during the First Millenia BC and AD*, DAJ, vol.8, 1992.

Fernie, E., *The Architecture of the Anglo-Saxons*, 1983.

Finucane, R., *The Posthumous Miracles of Godric of Finchale*, TAASDN, new series, vol.III, 1974.

Fisher, E.A., *The Greater Anglo-Saxon Churches*, 1962.

Fordyce, W., *The History and Antiquities of Durham*, vol.I, 1857.

Fowler, T., *Richard Fox*, DNB vol.XX, 1889.

Fraser, C.M., *A History of Antony Bek, Bishop of Durham 1283-1311*, 1957.

Fraser, C.M., and Emsley, K., *Durham and the wapentake of Sadberge*, TAASDN, new series vol.II, 1970.

Fraser, C.M., and Emsley, K., *Northumbria*, 2nd ed 1989

Garnett, O., *Souter Lighthouse and the Leas*, 1995.

Gee, H., *Ecclesiastical History*, VCH vol.II, 1907.

Gelling, M., *Signposts to the Past: Place-names and the History of England.* 2nd ed., 1988.

Gilbert, E., *Anglian remains at St Peter's, Monkwearmouth*, AA 4, vol.XXV, 1947.

Greenwell, W., *Durham Cathedral*, TAASDN, vol.II, 1883.

Halcrow, E.M., *Obedientaries and Counsellors in Monastic Administration at Durham*, AA 4, vol.XXXV, 1957.

Halsey, R., *The Galilee Chapel*, 'Medieval Art and Architecture at Durham Cathedral', 1980.

Harbottle, B., *Bishop Hatfield's visitation of Durham Priory in 1354*, AA 4, vol.XXXVI, 1958.

Harding, A.F., and Young, R., *Pictures of an Exhibition: new discoveries concerning the Heathery Burn Hoard.* DAJ, vol.II, 1986.

Harding, D.W., *County Durham in the Prehistoric Period*, TAASDN, new series vol.II, 1970.

Harrison, S.A., *Observations on the Architecture of the Galilee Chapel*, AND, 1993.

Hartley, B., and Fitts, L., *The Brigantes*, 1988.

Harvey, J., *The Medieval Architect*, 1972.

Haselgrove, C., and Healey, E., *The Prehistory of the Tyne-Tees Lowlands, Some Recent Finds*, DAJ, vol.8, 1992.

Hay, D., *The Dissolution of the Monasteries in the Diocese of Durham*, AA 4, vol.XV, 1938.

Higham, N., *The Northern Counties to AD 1000*, 1986.

Hislop, M., *The Castle of Ralph Fourth Baron Neville at Raby*, AA 5 vol. XX, 1992

Hugill, R., *Castles of Durham, 1979*.

Hunter Blair, C.H., *Knights of Durham who fought at the Battle of Lewes*, AA 4, vol.XXIV, 1946.

Hunter Blair, P., *The origins of Northumbria*, AA 4, vol.XXV, 1947.

Hunter Blair, P., *Northumbria in the days of Bede*, 1976.

Hunt, C.J., *The Lead Miners of the Northern Pennines in the eighteenth and nineteenth centuries*, 1970.

Hutchinson, W., *The History and Antiquities of the County Palatine of Durham*, vol.I, 1817.

Jarrett, M.G., and Edwards, B.J.N., *Medieval and other pottery from Finchale Priory, Co. Durham*, AA 4, vol.XXXIX, 1961.

Jensen, G.F., *The Vikings in England: a review*, 'Anglo-Saxon England' 4, 1975.

Jobey, G., *An Iron Age homestead at West Brandon, Durham*, AA 4, vol.XL, 1962.

Johnson, M., *The Great North Gate of Durham Castle*, TAASDN, new series, vol.IV, 1977.

Johnson, M., *The Washington Family in Britain*, 1985.

Jolliffe, J.E.A., *Northumbrian Institutions*, EHR, XLI, 1926.

Kapelle, W.E., *The Norman Conquest of the North*, 1979.

Kerr, N. and Kerr, M., *A Guide to Anglo-Saxon Sites*, 1982.

Kingsford, C.L., *Hugh du Puiset*, DNB vol.XLVII, 1896.

Lapsley, G.T., *The County Palatine of Durham: a study in Constitutional History*, 1900.

Lee, C.E., The Wagonways of Tyneside AA 4 vol.XXIX, 1951.

Lewis, M.J.T., *Early Wooden Railways*, 1970.

Linsley, S.M., *Ryhope Pumping Station: A History and Description*, 1973

Lomas, R., *The North East in the Middle Ages*, 1992.

Manby, T.G., *Neolithic pottery from Hasting Hill, County Durham*, AA 5, vol.I, 1973.

Mann, J.C., *Causey Arch - a note*, AA 5 vol. XII, 1984.

Matthew, D., *Durham and the Anglo-Norman World*, AND, 1993.

Mawer, A., *The Place-names of Northumberland and Durham*, 1920.

Mawer, A., *The river-names of Northumberland and Durham*, AA 4, vol.VI, 1929.

Mcaleer, J.P., *The West Front of Durham Cathedral: the Beginning of a British Tradition*, AND, 1993.

McKisack, M., *The Fourteenth Century: 1307-1399*, 1959.

Meyvaert, P., *Bede and the Church Paintings at Wearmouth-Jarrow*, 'Anglo-Saxon England', 8, 1979.

Milburn, G.E., *Holy Trinity Church*, 1992?

Morley, B.M., *Hylton Castle*, 1979.

Morris, C.D., *Northumbria and the Viking Settlement: the evidence for land-holding*, AA 5, vol.V, 1977.

Morris, C.D., *Aspects of Scandinavian Settlement in northern England: a review*, NH, vol.XX, 1984.

Offler, H.S., *Murder on Framwellgate Bridge*, AA 5 vol.XVI, 1988.

Osmond, P.H., *A Life of John Cosin: Bishop of Durham 1660-1672*, 1913.

Overton, J.H., *John Cosin*, DNB vol.XII, 1887.

Pearson, W., *Edwin, Coniscliffe and the Quest for Hela and 'Thorns,'* DAJ, vol.7, 1991.

Peers, C.R., *Finchale Priory*, AA 4, vol.IV, 1927.

Pevsner N, and Williamson, E., *County Durham*, 2nd ed., 1983.

Pollard, A.F., *Cuthbert Tunstall*, DNB vol. LVII, 1899.

Poole, R.L., *Thomas Hatfield*, DNB, vol.XXV, 1891.

Prestwich, M.C., *Edward I*, 1988.

Price, G., *The Languages of Britain*, 1984.

Quekett J., and Cheetham, F.H., *Architectural Description (Durham Cathedral)*, VCH vol.III, ed. W. Page, 1928.

Richardson, R.K., *The Bishopric of Durham under Antony Bek, 1283-1311*, AA 3, vol.IX, 1913.

Raistrick A., & Roberts, A., *Life and Work of the Northern Lead Miner*, 1984.

Rhodes, J.N., *Lead Mining and Smelting in County Durham*, 'The Great Age of Industry in the North East' (ed.) R.W. Sturgess, 1981.

Richley, M., *History of Bishop Auckland*, 1872.

Robinson, J.M., *The Architecture of Northern England*, 1986.

Rowley, T., *The Norman Heritage, 1066-1200*, 1983.

Salway, P., *The Frontier People of Roman Britain*, 1965.

Scammell, G.V., *Hugh du Puiset, Bishop of Durham*, 1956.

Scammell, J., *The Origin and Limitations of the Liberty of Durham*, EHR, LXXXI, 1966.

Smith, H.J., *The Sunderland and South Shields Water Company*, SH 3, 1985.

Stenton, F.M., *Anglo-Saxon England*, 3rd ed., 1971.

Storey, R.L., *Thomas Langley and the Bishopric of Durham, 1406-1437*, 1961.

Stranks, C.J., *This Sumptuous Church: the story of Durham Cathedral*, 1973.

Sturge, C., *Cuthbert Tunstal*, 1938.

Surtees, R., *The History and Antiquities of the County palatine of Durham*, vols.I-IV, 1816-40.

Thorold, H., *County Durham, 1980*.

Thurlby, M., *The Roles of the Patron and the Master Mason in the First Design of the Romanesque Cathedral of Durham*, AND, 1993.

Tudor, V., *The Misogyny of St Cuthbert*, AA 5, vol.XII, 1984.

Tudor, V., *Durham Priory and its Hermits in the Twelfth Century*, AND, 1993.

Washington, G.S.H.L., *The earliest Washingtons and their Anglo-Scottish connections, 1964*.

Webb, G., *Architecture in Britain: the Middle Ages*, 1956.

Whiting, C.E., *Richard de Bury, Bishop of Durham*, TAASDN, vol.X, 1954.

Wills, M., *Gibside and the Bowes Family*, 1995

Wilson, C., *The Neville Screen*, 'Art and Architecture at Durham Cathedral', 1980.

Wormald, P., *The Age of Bede and Aethelbald*, 'The Anglo-Saxons', ed., J. Campbell, 1982.

Young, A., *William Cumin: Border Politics and the Bishopric of Durham, 1141-1144*, 1979

Young, R., *Fieldwork and Excavation at the Crawley Edge Cairnfield, Stanhope, Co. Durham*, DAJ, vol.8, 1992.

INDEX

PICTURE CREDITS

Shaun Dodds, Nos 5, 7, 10, 20, 24 (courtesy of University College, Durham), 28, 34, 35, 36, 40, 49, 50, 51, 52, 58, 60, 61, 62, 64, 69, 70, 75, 76, 78, 79

Gavin Dodds, Nos Cover, 1, 11, 12, 13, 17, 18, 19, 23, 38, 42, 43, 45, 46, 53, 54, 56, 66, 71, 72, 73, 77

Robert Surtees, *The History and Antiquities of the County Palatine of Durham*, vols. I-IV, 1816-1840, Nos 3, 21, 25, 33, 44

Robert Billings, *Illustrations of the Architectural Antiquities of the County of Durham*, 1846, Nos 6, 26, 32, 39, 55

University of Newcastle upon Tyne, Nos 14, 29, 37, 47, 59

Pitkin Pictorials Ltd., Nos 30, 31

Sunderland Antiquarian Society, Nos 4, 57

Courtesy of The Bowes Museum, No. 15

Courtesy of George Edwards of the Ryhope Engines Trust, Nos 65, 67

Courtesy of the Society of Antiquaries of Newcastle upon Tyne, No. 74

James Paine, *Plans, Elevations and Sections of Noblemen and Gentlemen's Houses*, volume I, 1767, No. 41

English Heritage, Nos 8, 9

The Builder, 14th Jan. 1871, No. 16

University College, Durham, Nos 22, 27

National Trust, No. 68

English Life, (courtesy of the Lord Barnard), No. 63

Department of Archaeology, University of Durham, No. 2